DEPARTMENT OF THE NAVY
HEADQUARTERS UNITED STATES MARINE CORPS
3000 MARINE CORPS PENTAGON
WASHINGTON, DC 20350-3000

MARINE CORPS MANAGEMENT AND USE OF THE ELECTROMAGNETIC SPECTRUM

DEPARTMENT OF THE NAVY
HEADQUARTERS UNITED STATES MARINE CORPS
3000 MARINE CORPS PENTAGON
WASHINGTON, DC 20350-3000

MCO 2400.2A
C4
7 Oct 2009

MARINE CORPS ORDER 2400.2A

From: Commandant of the Marine Corps
To: Distribution List

Subj: MARINE CORPS MANAGEMENT AND USE OF THE ELECTROMAGNETIC
       SPECTRUM

Ref: (a) SECNAVINST 2400.1
       (b) Office of Management and Budget (OMB) Circular A-11,
           "Preparation, Submission and Execution of the Budget,
           Part 3," June 2008
       (c) National Telecommunications and Information
           Administration (NTIA), "Manual of Regulations and
           Procedures for Federal Radio Frequency Management
           (Redbook)," January 2009
       (d) DODD 5000.01, "The Defense Acquisition System," May
           12, 2003
       (e) DODI 4650.01, "Policy and Procedures for Management of
           Use of the Electromagnetic Spectrum," January 9, 2009
       (f) DODI 5000.02, "Operation of the Defense Acquisition
           System," December 8, 2008
       (g) OPNAVINST 2400.20F
       (h) ACP 190 U.S. SUPP-1(D), "Guide to Frequency Planning,"
           September 1, 2001
       (i) DODD 3222.3, "DOD Electromagnetic Environmental Effects
           (E3) Program," September 8, 2004
       (j) MCO 2410.2B
       (k) DODI 5200.01, "DOD Information Security Program and
           Protection of Sensitive Compartmental Information,"
           October 9, 2008
       (l) Joint Staff Memorandum, "Designation of Spectrum XXI
           as the Joint Standard Frequency Assignment System,"
           dtd 29 Jul 05 (NOTAL)
       (m) CJCSI 3320.03A, "Joint Communications Electronics
           Operation Instructions," June 1, 2005
       (n) Joint Staff Memorandum, "Designation of JACS as the
           Joint Staff Communications Electronics Operations
           Instruction (CEOI) Generation Tool," dtd 6 Jan 05
           (NOTAL)

DISTRIBUTION STATEMENT A: Approved for public release;
distribution is unlimited.

(o) "DOD Frequency Assignment and Equipment Spectrum Certification Security Classification Guide," November 30, 2007 (NOTAL)

(p) Military Communications-Electronics Board (MCEB) PUB 7, "Frequency Resource Record System (FRRS) Standard Frequency Action Format (SFAF)," June 30, 2005

(q) Communications Act of 1934 (further amended by the Telecommunications Act of 1996)

(r) CJCSM 3320.01B, "Joint Operations in the Electromagnetic Battlespace," March 25, 2006

(s) CJCSM 3212.02B, "Performing Electronic Attack in the United States and Canada for Tests, Training and Exercises," October 15, 2003 (NOTAL)

(t) CJCSI 3320.02C-1, "Classified Supplement to Joint Spectrum Interference Resolution (JSIR) Procedures," December 17, 2008 (NOTAL)

(u) CJCSI 3320.02D, "Joint Spectrum Interference Resolution (JSIR)," January 9, 2009

(v) CJCSM 3320.02B, "Joint Spectrum Interference Resolution (JSIR) Procedures," December 31, 2008

(w) 47, U.S.C.

(x) JANAP 119(M), "Joint Voice Call Sign Book," October 2004 (NOTAL)

(y) SECNAV M-5210.1

Encl: (1) Marine Corps Management and Use of the Electromagnetic Spectrum Guidance

1. Situation. Based upon operational requirements and emerging technology, the Marine Corps has experienced a proliferation of spectrum-dependent (S-D) equipment and systems, which provide critical command and control (C2); intelligence, surveillance and reconnaissance (ISR) functions; and electronic warfare (EW) capabilities across the operating forces. These S-D equipment and systems are no longer isolated solely within the communications community, but span and connect the Marine Air Ground Task Force (MAGTF) across the strategic, operational, and tactical levels of warfare. Fully understanding the operational necessity of effectively and efficiently managing the electromagnetic spectrum is critical to the Marine Corps ability to utilize, control, and exploit this critically saturated, finite resource during current and future operations.

2. Cancellation. MCO 2400.2 and MCO 2345.1.

3. <u>Mission</u>. This Order establishes policy, guidance, and procedures for the effective and efficient management of the electromagnetic spectrum and identifies specific command relationships, roles, and responsibilities in the proper management and employment of S-D equipment and systems in support of the Marine Corps Operating Forces (OPFOR), installations, organizations, and activities in accordance with references (a) through (y).

4. Execution

   a. <u>Commander's Intent and Concept of Operations</u>

   (1) <u>Commander's Intent</u>. The Marine Corps will effectively and efficiently manage the electromagnetic spectrum and ensure the Marine Corps provides equipment, capabilities, and services to the OPFOR and Supporting Establishment that enable commanders to utilize S-D equipment and systems in the successful completion of their assigned missions. Consideration of the electromagnetic spectrum and operational environment is critical to acquisition, operations, and sustainment and must continually be evaluated across the strategic, operational, and tactical planning levels of the MAGTF to ensure effective employment in the numerous and various locations in which the Marine Corps deploys. Marine Corps management and use of the electromagnetic spectrum must be guided by international, national, Department of Defense (DoD) and Department of Navy (DON) policy and regulations, while also providing flexible and responsive support to Marine Corps operations and training. Through streamlined policy and coordinated efforts, Marine Corps management and use of the electromagnetic spectrum will effectively and successfully support Marine Corps operational requirements.

   (2) <u>Concept of Operations</u>

   (a) In accordance with reference (a), the Commandant of the Marine Corps (CMC) is responsible for the Marine Corps management and use of the electromagnetic spectrum and exercises operational authority by providing command structure and resources to ensure spectrum access to the MAGTF.

   (b) The Director, Command, Control, Communications and Computers (C4), Headquarters, U.S. Marine Corps (HQMC)/ DON Deputy Chief Information Officer (CIO) Marine Corps (DDCIO(MC)), provides Marine Corps electromagnetic spectrum policy and oversees spectrum use, requirements, and operations.

(c) Marine Corps Systems Command (MARCORSYSCOM) provides supervision and management of the spectrum supportability and certification process throughout all phases of the acquisition lifecycle to ensure seamless integration of S-D equipment and systems into the electromagnetic environment (EME) in support of the Marine Corps OPFOR, installations, organizations and activities.

(d) OPFOR commanders (e.g., U.S. Marine Corps Forces (MARFOR), Marine Expeditionary Forces (MEF), Major Subordinate Commands (MSC), etc.) and commanders of Marine Corps Installations (MCI) (e.g., bases, posts, stations, and installations) provide oversight, supervision and management of the operational, training, day-to-day requirements and use of the electromagnetic spectrum.

(e) S-D equipment and systems are defined as any conceptual, experimental, developmental or operational transmitter, receiver or device (unclassified or classified) that utilizes any portion or part of the electromagnetic spectrum. S-D equipment and systems include, but are not limited to transmitters, receivers, Command and Control (C2) systems and platforms (including satellite communications (SATCOM)), ISR systems and platforms (either manned or unmanned), EW assets, sensors, beacons, navigational aids (NAVAIDS), radar, lasers, munitions, and weapons systems. There is no distinction as to the method of procurement to include program and non-program of record; Government-developed or Government-off-the shelf (GOTS); commercial-off-the-shelf (COTS); commercial lease; or operations and maintenance (O&M)/unit funded.

(f) Ensure effective and efficient spectrum management is considered at all levels of Marine Corps operational planning to ensure access to the electromagnetic spectrum in support of Marine Corps OPFOR, installations, organizations and activities.

(g) Ensure spectrum supportability is considered early and during all phases of the acquisition process for the proper development, procurement, and fielding of S-D equipment and systems to the Marine Corps OPFOR, installations, organizations, and activities to include Host Nation Authorization (HNA) for operational spectrum requirements Outside the United States and Possessions (OUS&P).

4

(h) Advocate and invest in the development of new and emergent spectrum efficient technologies in support of Marine Corps operational requirements.

(3) <u>Subordinate Element Missions</u>

(a) <u>Director, C4/DDCIO(MC))</u>

<u>1</u>. Establish Marine Corps spectrum policy, guidance and procedures for the effective and efficient management of the electromagnetic spectrum.

<u>2</u>. Provide oversight and administration of Marine Corps policy, management and use of the electromagnetic spectrum, spectrum requirements, and operations.

<u>3</u>. Ensure Marine Corps compliance with applicable international, national, DoD, Joint and DON statutory and regulatory policies.

<u>4</u>. Serve as the principle advisor to the DoD, Joint Staff, and other Governmental agencies in support of Marine Corps Service related issues regarding the electromagnetic spectrum, spectrum requirements and operations.

<u>5</u>. Coordinate Marine Corps administrative and operational spectrum management support requirements with the Secretary of the Navy (SECNAV) and other Military Departments (MILDEPS) and Service Chiefs as required.

<u>a</u>. Support the DON at the Interdepartment Radio Advisory Committee (IRAC) of the National Telecommunications and Information Administration (NTIA).

<u>b</u>. Serve as the principle Marine Corps member to the Military Communications-Electronics Board (MCEB) Frequency Panel (FP) and associated working groups and forums and designate and delegate Marine Corps representation, as required, in support of Marine Corps use of the electromagnetic spectrum, spectrum requirements and operations.

<u>6</u>. Provide administrative oversight of the Marine Corps spectrum supportability and certification process in support of Marine Corps Systems Command (MARCORSYSCOM) program offices (PO); Joint Program Offices (JPO) where the Marine Corps is the Executive Agent (EA); Marine Corps Warfighting Lab (MCWL); procurements by the Marine Corps OPFOR, installations, organizations and activities; and other

supporting entities for spectrum supportability, certification and host nation coordination (HNC) issues during the acquisition process.

       <u>7</u>. Assign responsibilities to and coordinate Marine Corps administrative and operational spectrum management support requirements with the Navy and Marine Corps Spectrum Center (NMSC) and regional Navy and Marine Corps Spectrum Offices (NMCSO) within the US&P as required.

       <u>8</u>. Coordinate and assign Marine Corps administrative and operational spectrum management support requirements with MILDEP and regional spectrum offices within US&P as required (e.g., DoD Area Frequency Coordinators (AFC), etc.).

       <u>9</u>. Coordinate and provide administrative and operational spectrum management support, as required, to the Marine Corps OPFOR, installations, organizations and activities in support of spectrum management operational requirements.

       <u>10</u>. Coordinate Marine Corps administrative and operational spectrum management support requirements with the Marine Corps Service Components (i.e., MARFOR) in support of regional Combatant Commands (COCOM), as required, to include HNC.

       <u>11</u>. Coordinate and provide administrative and technical support, as required, to the Marine Corps OPFOR, installations, organizations and activities during the Service level and Joint Spectrum Interference Resolution (JSIR) processes.

       <u>12</u>. Provide appropriate mechanisms to the Marine Corps OPFOR, installations, organizations and activities, whereby compliance with the provisions of this Order are understood, administered, and validated.

      (b) <u>Commander, MARCORSYSCOM</u>

       <u>1</u>. Act as the focal point for and provide administrative and technical support to MARCORSYSCOM PO; JPO where the Marine Corps is the EA; MCWL; procurements by the Marine Corps OPFOR; installations and other entities for spectrum supportability, certification and HNC issues during the acquisition process.

<u>2</u>. Ensure spectrum supportability, certification and electromagnetic environmental effects (E3) are considered as early as possible in the acquisition process and in parallel with other acquisition activities.

<u>3</u>. Coordinate Marine Corps administrative and operational spectrum management support requirements, as required, during the spectrum supportability and certification process with the NMSC and regional NMCSOs within US&P to include coordinating and obtaining frequency assignments in support of testing, evaluation and demonstration of S-D equipment and systems during the acquisition process.

<u>4</u>. Coordinate Marine Corps administrative and operational spectrum management support requirements, as required, with the Marine Corps Service Components (i.e., MARFOR) in support of the regional COCOM to include HNC.

<u>5</u>. Provide policy, guidance and procedures to the PO and Program Managers (PM) during the acquisition process to ensure the proper and sufficient documentation of S-D equipment and systems technical characteristics and parameters, submission and tracking of NTIA certification and note-to holders (NTH), and host nation authorization (HNA) packages.

<u>a</u>. Timely publication and dissemination of NTIA certification documentation (e.g., approved DD-1494 or J/F 12) within the appropriate databases.

<u>b</u>. Audit and deletion of legacy and obsolete S-D equipment and systems within the appropriate databases when no longer in the Marine Corps inventory.

<u>c</u>. Host Nation Coordination.

<u>d</u>. Provide annual training to PO/PM on the spectrum supportability processes and procedures and develop, provide and maintain documentation, checklists, etc. in support of this effort.

<u>6</u>. Advocate and invest in the development of new and emergent spectrum efficient technologies in support of Marine Corps operational requirements.

(c) <u>Commanders, U.S. Marine Corps Forces (MARFOR)</u>

<u>1</u>.   Establish MARFOR level spectrum policy, guidance, and procedures for the effective and efficient management and use of the electromagnetic spectrum.

<u>a</u>.   Ensure effective and efficient spectrum management is considered at all levels of Marine Corps operational planning to ensure access to the electromagnetic spectrum in support of the Marine Corps OPFOR, installations, organizations and activities.

<u>b</u>.   Provide procedures for the planning, assignment, coordination, deconfliction and utilization of the electromagnetic spectrum.

<u>c</u>.   Provide procedures for the timely and accurate identification, reporting, and resolution of electromagnetic interference (EMI) for assured access to the electromagnetic spectrum.

<u>2</u>.   Provide oversight and administration of MARFOR policy, management and use of the electromagnetic spectrum, spectrum requirements and operations.

<u>3</u>.   Ensure MARFOR compliance with applicable international, national, DoD, Joint, DON and Marine Corps statutory and regulatory policies.

<u>4</u>.   Ensure spectrum supportability, certification and HNC/HNA is validated/completed for S-D equipment and systems prior to operational use.

<u>5</u>.   Coordinate and provide administrative and operational spectrum management support, as required, to Marine Corps OPFOR, installations, organizations and activities in support of spectrum management operational requirements to include coordination with the NMSC and regional NMCSOs within US&P as required.

<u>6</u>.   Coordinate Marine Corps administrative and operational spectrum management support requirements in support of regional COCOM, as required, to include HNC.

<u>7</u>.   Coordinate and provide administrative and technical support to Marine Corps OPFOR, installations, organizations and activities during the Service level and Joint Spectrum Interference Resolution (JSIR) processes.

8

(d) <u>Commanders, Marine Expeditionary Forces (MEF)</u>

<u>1</u>. Establish MEF level spectrum policy, guidance and procedures for the effective and efficient management of the electromagnetic spectrum.

<u>a</u>. Ensure effective and efficient spectrum management is considered at all levels of MAGTF operational planning to ensure access to the electromagnetic spectrum in support of the Marine Corps OPFOR.

<u>b</u>. Provide procedures for the planning, assignment, coordination, deconfliction and utilization of the electromagnetic spectrum.

<u>c</u>. Provide procedures for the timely and accurate identification, reporting, and resolution of EMI for assured access to the electromagnetic spectrum.

<u>2</u>. Provide oversight and administration of MEF policy, management and use of the electromagnetic spectrum, spectrum requirements and operations.

<u>3</u>. Ensure MEF compliance with applicable international, national, DoD, Joint, DON and Marine Corps statutory and regulatory policies.

<u>4</u>. Ensure spectrum supportability, certification and HNC/HNA is validated/completed for S-D equipment and systems prior to operational use.

<u>5</u>. Coordinate and provide administrative and operational spectrum management support, as required, to the Marine Corps OPFOR in support of spectrum management operational requirements to include coordination with regional NMCSOs within US&P as required.

<u>6</u>. Coordinate Marine Corps administrative and operational spectrum management support requirements in support of regional COCOM, as required, to include HNC.

<u>7</u>. Coordinate and provide administrative and technical support to the Marine Corps OPFOR during the Service level and Joint Spectrum Interference Resolution (JSIR) processes.

(e) <u>Commanding Generals, Marine Corps Installations</u> (MCI)

<u>1</u>. Establish MCI level spectrum policy, guidance, and procedures for the effective and efficient management of the electromagnetic spectrum.

<u>a</u>. Ensure effective and efficient spectrum management is considered at all levels of operational planning to ensure access to the electromagnetic spectrum in support of Marine Corps installations, organizations and activities.

<u>b</u>. Provide procedures for the planning, assignment, coordination, deconfliction and utilization of the electromagnetic spectrum.

<u>c</u>. Provide procedures for the timely and accurate identification, reporting, and resolution of EMI for assured access to the electromagnetic spectrum.

<u>2</u>. Provide oversight and administration of MCI policy, management and use of the electromagnetic spectrum, spectrum requirements and operations.

<u>3</u>. Ensure MCI compliance with applicable international, national, DoD, Joint, DON and Marine Corps statutory and regulatory policies.

<u>4</u>. Ensure spectrum supportability, certification and HNC/HNA is validated/completed for S-D equipment and systems prior to operational use.

<u>5</u>. Coordinate and provide administrative and operational spectrum management support, as required, to Marine Corps installations, organizations and activities in support of spectrum management operational requirements to include coordination with regional NMCSOs within US&P as required.

<u>6</u>. Coordinate Marine Corps administrative and operational spectrum management support requirements in support of regional COCOM, as required, to include HNC.

<u>7</u>. Coordinate and provide administrative and technical support to MCIs, organizations and activities during the Service level and Joint Spectrum Interference Resolution (JSIR) processes.

  c. <u>Coordinating Instructions</u>. Coordinating instructions are contained within enclosure (1) of this Order.

5. <u>Administration and Logistics</u>. Submit recommended changes to this Order, with complete justification, to Commandant of the Marine Corps (Dir, C4), via the chain of command.

6. <u>Command and Signal</u>

  a. <u>Command</u>. This Order is applicable to the Marine Corps Total Force.

  b. <u>Signal</u>. This Order is effective the date signed.

W. J. WILLIAMS
Director, Marine Corps Staff

DISTRIBUTION: PCN 10202872400

LOCATOR PAGE

Subj: MARINE CORPS MANAGEMENT OF THE ELECTROMAGNETIC SPECTRUM

Location: _____

(Indicate the location(s) of the copy(ies) of this
Order.)

RECORD OF CHANGES

Log completed change action as indicated.

Change Number	Date of Change	Date Entered	Signature of Person Incorporated Change

TABLE OF CONTENTS

Chapter 1

Organization

1. <u>International</u>. The International Telecommunication Union (ITU) was established in 1865 and is the leading United Nations (UN) agency for information and communication technologies. As the global focal point for Governments and the private sector, the ITU's role in helping the world communicate spans three core sectors: radiocommunication, standardization and development. The ITU is based in Geneva, Switzerland, and its membership includes 191 Member States and more than 700 Sector Members and Associates. The goals of the ITU are to:

a. Maintain and extend international cooperation for the improvement and rational use of telecommunications of all kinds.

b. Establish international rules and regulations that are ratified by the member nations.

c. Promote the development of technical facilities and their efficient operation with a view of improving the efficiency of telecommunications service.

d. Harmonize the actions of nations in the attainment of these goals.

2. <u>National (Federal Government)</u>. The National Telecommunications and Information Administration (NTIA), a bureau of the U.S. Department of Commerce (DOC), is the President of the United State's principal adviser on telecommunications and information policy issues, and works with other Executive Branch agencies to develop and present the Administration's position on these issues. NTIA manages the Federal Government's use of the electromagnetic spectrum; performs telecommunications research and engineering; and administers infrastructure and public telecommunications facilities grants.

a. <u>Office of Spectrum Management (OSM)</u>. The OSM is responsible for managing the Federal Government's use of the electromagnetic spectrum. To achieve this, the OSM receives assistance and advice from the Interdepartment Radio Advisory Committee (IRAC). The OSM carries out this responsibility by:

(1) Establishing and issuing policy regarding allocations and regulations governing the Federal spectrum use.

(2) Developing plans for peacetime and wartime use of the electromagnetic spectrum.

(3) Preparing for, participating in, and implementing the results of international radio conferences.

(4) Assigning of frequencies.

(5) Maintenance of spectrum use databases.

(6) Reviewing Federal agencies' new telecommunications systems and certifying that spectrum will be available.

(7) Providing technical engineering expertise required to perform specific spectrum resource assessments and automated computer capabilities needed to carry out these investigations.

(8) Participates in all aspects of the Federal Government's communications related emergency readiness activities.

(9) Participates in Federal Government telecommunications and automated information systems security activities.

b. Interdepartment Radio Advisory Committee (IRAC). The purpose of the IRAC is to assign frequencies to U.S. Government radio stations and develop and execute policies, programs, procedures and technical criteria pertaining to the allocation, management, and use of the electromagnetic spectrum within the United States and Possessions (US&P). The IRAC consists of a main committee, subcommittees and ad-hoc working groups that consider various aspects of spectrum management policy.

(1) The IRAC main committee consists of representatives appointed by each of the following member departments and agencies:

(a) Department of Agriculture

(b) Department of the Air Force

(c) Department of the Army

(d) Broadcasting Board of Governors

(e) United States Coast Guard

(f) Department of Commerce

(g) Department of Energy

(h) Federal Aviation Administration

(i) Department of Homeland Security

(j) Department of the Interior

(k) Department of Justice

(l) National Aeronautics and Space Administration

(m) National Science Foundation

(n) Department of the Navy

(o) Department of State

(p) Department of Transportation

(q) Department of Treasury

(r) United States Postal Service

(s) Veterans Affairs

(2) The IRAC's substructure consists of the:

(a) <u>Frequency Assignment Subcommittee (FAS)</u>. The FAS consists of a representative appointed by each of the 19 IRAC departments/agencies and acts as the assignment and coordination authority of radio frequencies for the Federal Government and the development and execution of procedures relating to these functions. Liaison between the FAS and the Federal Communications Commission (FCC) is affected by FCC Representation on the FAS. Normal frequency assignment actions are addressed by voting on a daily basis. Requests for radio licenses and many problems are resolved by coordination among the affected Government agencies representatives. Frequency assignment issues; problems that cannot be resolved by local coordination; and improvements and refinements to the frequency assignment process are addressed monthly by the FAS.

(b) <u>Spectrum Planning Subcommittee (SPS)</u>. The SPS consists of a representative appointed by each of the 19 IRAC departments/agencies and is responsible for carrying out those functions that relate to the planning and use of the electromagnetic spectrum in the National interest; the apportionment of spectrum space for established or anticipated radio services; the apportionment of spectrum space between or among Government and non-Federal activities; and other matters as the IRAC may direct. Liaison between the SPS and the FCC is affected by the FCC representation on the SPS. The SPS:

<u>1</u>. Maintains and makes recommendations for changes in the Table of Frequency Allocations or other actions, as appropriate; new developments in existing services; new techniques, the application of which may require revision of the Table of Frequency Allocations; new services for which the current table makes no provisions; specific proposals for expansion, reduction, or other changes in the allocated frequency bands; and the international aspects of changes recommended to the IRAC.

<u>2</u>. Ensures electromagnetic compatibility (EMC) among electronic systems and observance in accordance with the NTIA Manual of Regulations and Procedures for Federal Radio Frequency Management.

<u>3</u>. Develops procedures enabling the maintenance of pertinent documentation of planned and operational satellite systems including their technical and operational characteristics.

<u>4</u>. Ascertains system concept development, where compatibility may not exist and make recommendations as to potential EMC problem areas, and proposes courses of action to resolve these problems.

<u>5</u>. Makes recommendations as to technical parameters necessary to facilitate sharing between systems; reviews effectiveness of existing systems with a view toward rectifying compatibility deficiencies.

(c) <u>Emergency Planning Subcommittee (EPS)</u>. The EPS formulates, guides and reviews National Security Emergency Preparedness (NSEP) planning for Federal spectrum-dependent (S-D) equipment and systems.

(d) <u>Radio Conference Subcommittee (RCS)</u>. The RCS consists of a representative appointed by each of the 19 IRAC departments/agencies and is responsible for carrying out those functions given in Article II that relate to preparing for ITU conferences, including the ITU Plenipotentiary Conferences, ITU

Radio-Communication Assembly (RCA), council as it pertains to matters involving radio, and the Radiocommunication Advisory Group including the development of recommended U.S. proposals and positions. The RCS focuses on current and planned national and international frequency uses, and optimum placement of radio services to ensure effective use of the spectrum in the overall national interest; anticipated needs of all radio services; new developments in existing services; new techniques, the application of which may require revision of regulations concerning radio frequency matters; and new services for which the current regulations makes no provisions.

(e) Space Systems Subcommittee (SSS). The SSS is responsible for international registration of Government satellite systems within the ITU forum and acts on behalf of the IRAC to coordinate with the Deputy Associate Administrator, OSM to review, modify, develop, and maintain the procedures for national implementation of space related provisions of the ITU Radio Regulations; advance publish, coordinate, and notify Government space systems under the applicable provisions of the ITU Radio Regulations; respond to the data furnished by other administrations and the Radiocommunication Bureau regarding proposed space telecommunications systems in accordance with the applicable provisions of the ITU Radio Regulations. Liaison between the SSS and the Federal Communications Commission (FCC) is affected by the FCC Representation on the SSS.

(f) Technical Subcommittee (TSC). The TSC assists NTIA in addressing issues that relate to the technical aspects of the use of the electromagnetic spectrum, as well as such other matters as directed by the IRAC. The TSC evaluates current and proposed efforts regarding the adequacy of the technical bases for spectrum management; the effectiveness of specific programs with regard to improved use of the spectrum; the need for new criteria, procedures, and methodologies for use of the spectrum. TSC assistance to NTIA includes:

1. Development of recommendations concerning new technical standards and improvement of existing standards pertaining to use of the radio spectrum.

2. Maintaining awareness of the radio propagation (including natural radio noise) programs and needs of the Government for purposes of evaluating and making recommendations leading to a better utilization of the radio spectrum.

_3_. Providing evaluations and recommendations, in the form of technical reports, on new and existing techniques and their ability to optimize use of the radio spectrum, including implementation steps.

_4_. Providing evaluations and recommendations, in the form of technical reports, regarding the EMC capabilities and needs of the Government in support of spectrum management, including techniques and criteria leading to greater inter- and intra-radio service sharing of available spectrum and the reduction of man-made radio noise.

3. National (Non-Federal Government) Federal Communications Commission (FCC). The FCC is an independent United States Government agency established by the Communications Act of 1934 (as amended by the Telecommunications Act of 1996) and charged with regulating all non-Federal Government use of the radio frequency spectrum (including radio and television broadcasting); all interstate telecommunications (wire, satellite and cable); and all international communications that originate or terminate in the United States. It is an important factor in U.S. telecommunication policy.

a. The FCC's jurisdiction covers the 50 states, the District of Columbia, and all U.S. possessions.

b. The FCC rules and regulations are codified in Title 47 of the United States Code (U.S.C.).

4. Department of Defense (DOD)

a. Secretary of Defense (SECDEF). The SECDEF is responsible for all acquisition, operations, and resources utilizing the electromagnetic spectrum within the Department of Defense (DOD).

(1) The Assistant Secretary of Defense for Networks and Information Integration (ASD(NII)). The ASD(NII) provides policy, oversight and guidance for all DOD matters related to the management and use of the electromagnetic spectrum and electromagnetic environmental effects (E3). ASD(NII) represents and coordinates DOD positions within international, regional, national and Federal Government spectrum management organizations and forums in support of DOD policy and standards.

b. Joint Chiefs of Staff (JCS)

    (1) Director, Command, Control, Communications and Computer Systems, Joint Staff (J6). The J6 provides policy, procedures and operational support to the SECDEF, JCS, Services and DOD Components in support of Joint warfighting efforts. The J6 serves as the Joint Staff Spectrum Manager and advises the Chairman, Joint Chiefs of Staff (CJCS) on all spectrum matters; assists ASD(NII) in formulating policy and strategic planning, supports the COCOMs operational requirements.

    (2) Military Communications-Electronics Board (MCEB). The MCEB is chartered by ASD(NII) to coordinate military communications-electronics matters, including information technology (IT) and National Security Systems (NSS) to provide advice and assistance to the DOD components; between DOD and other Government departments and agencies; and between DOD and representatives of foreign nations. The MCEB is chaired by the Director for Command, Control, Communications and Computer Systems, Joint Staff with members and representatives comprising the DOD Components and Military Departments and Services.

        a. MCEB Frequency Panel (FP). Spectrum related functions of the MCEB fall under the cognizance of the, which provides expert technical advice to the MCEB in the areas of radio frequency engineering and electromagnetic spectrum management.

        b. The following permanent working groups are established/chartered under the FP to accomplish this mission:

        1. Spectrum Operations Permanent Working Group (SOPWG) provides guidance and procedures for the management and system enhancements of the Frequency Resource Record System (FRRS).

        2. Equipment Spectrum Guidance Permanent Working Group (ESGPWG) provides coordinated military guidance to the DOD components on spectrum dependent (S-D) equipment and systems in accordance with applicable DOD Directives, Allied, U.S. national, and international rules, regulations, and standards on spectrum management.

        3. Spectrum Management Architecture Permanent Working Group (SMAPWG) guides the development of a spectrum management architecture for the DOD spectrum management community.

<u>4</u>. International Telecommunications Union (ITU) Permanent Working Group (ITUPWG) establishes and executes a cohesive international spectrum management strategy for the ITU and related forums that address matters related to the management and use of the electromagnetic spectrum.

<u>5</u>. Allied Permanent Working Group (APWG) establishes and executes a cohesive international spectrum management strategy for regional and/or allied forums that address matters related to military management and use of the electromagnetic spectrum.

<u>6</u>. Space Systems Permanent Working Group (SSPWG) provides guidance and procedures on space system frequency matters.

<u>7</u>. Allotment Plan Management Permanent Working Group (APMPWG) provides spectrum related guidance for DOD fixed and mobile operations.

<u>8</u>. Dynamic Spectrum Access Permanent Working Group (DSAPWG) identifies, studies, and advises the FP on spectrum policy, regulations, standardization and doctrinal issues concerning DOD acquisition and deployment of communications-electronics equipment employing DSA and related technologies including wireless ad hoc mobile networking, software defined and cognitive radios.

(3) <u>Unified Combatant Command (COCOM)</u>. The Combatant Commander (CCDR) is responsible for the policy and use of the electromagnetic spectrum by U.S. Forces within their respective areas of responsibility (AOR) to include the coordination of frequency assignments and spectrum supportability with Allied and host nations; development and maintenance of the Joint Restricted Frequency List (JRFL) and Joint Communications-Electronics Operations Instruction (JCEOI); and other spectrum related processes uniquely applied to their AOR.

(a) <u>Joint Frequency Management Office (JFMO)</u>. The JFMO implements and executes COCOM policy and use of the electromagnetic spectrum. The JFMO provides:

<u>1</u>. Operational and contingency communications planning which consider and coordinate spectrum use among participating U.S., Joint and Coalition forces to enable information exchange, eliminate duplications of effort and achieve mutual support.

<u>2</u>. Necessary augmentation, coordination and support between the JFMO and the Joint Spectrum Management Element (JSME).

<u>3</u>. Resolves spectrum user conflicts.

<u>4</u>. Controlling authority for the JCEOI.

(b) <u>Joint Spectrum Management Element (JSME)</u>. The JSME is established by the Joint Force Commander (JFC) and provides policy, guidance and coordination between the JTF and the JFMO to include policy and guidance for the use of the electromagnetic spectrum, JRFL, JCEOI, and other spectrum related processes uniquely applied to the JTF. The JSME ensures assigned JTF forces are authorized sufficient use of the electromagnetic spectrum to execute their designated missions.

c. <u>Defense Spectrum Organization (DSO)</u>. The DSO, a Defense Information Systems Agency (DISA) entity, provides spectrum analysis and the development of integrated spectrum plans and long-term strategies to address current and future needs for DOD spectrum access. DSO provides direct operational support to the JCS, CCDRs, Secretaries of Military Departments (MILDEP), and Directors of Defense Agencies to achieve national security and military objectives.

(1) <u>Strategic Planning Office (SPO)</u>. The SPO works to transform spectrum management to support future net-centric operations and warfare. The SPO develops comprehensive and integrated spectrum planning strategies for the DOD, to support national spectrum planning efforts as well as DOD requirements and acquisition processes. The SPO:

(a) Ensures DOD is prepared to respond to international spectrum management issues and enhance the DOD's global spectrum access.

(b) Develops DOD strategies, for presentation to spectrum bodies within international organizations (e.g., the ITU, regional bodies, and North Atlantic Treaty Organization (NATO)).

(c) Promotes effective and efficient spectrum access technologies, key strategic alliances with Government, industry, and academia to maximize DOD spectrum utilization to meet mission requirements.

(2) <u>Joint Spectrum Center (JSC)</u>. The JSC, a field office within the DSO, provides expertise in the areas of spectrum planning, E3, information systems, modeling and simulation, and operations to provide complete, spectrum-related services directly to the JCS, CCDRs, MILDEPs, and Director's of Defense Agencies. JSC support provides:

(a) Electromagnetic environmental databases and analysis tools to assist in both the acquisition and operation of DOD communications-electronics assets.

(b) Engineering expertise and services dedicated to ensuring effective use of the electromagnetic spectrum.

(c) Services such as spectrum-planning guidance, system integration, system vulnerability analysis, environmental analysis, test and measurement support, operational support and spectrum management software development.

(d) Support for spectrum planning, spectrum certification of new weapon and sensor system development, and training and operational support to the unified commands, military departments, and defense agencies.

5. <u>Department of the Navy (DON)</u>

a. <u>Secretary of the Navy (SECNAV)</u>. The SECNAV is responsible for all acquisition, operations, resources and use of the electromagnetic spectrum within the DON in order to:

(1) Ensure sufficient spectrum is available to accomplish warfighting missions.

(2) Ensure efficient spectrum use.

(3) Promote spectrum efficient technologies with other public/private sector interests toward effective management of spectrum resources.

(4) Influence the development of national level spectrum positions and policies.

b. <u>Department of the Navy, Chief Information Officer (DON CIO)</u>. DON CIO is responsible to the SECNAV for all national and international spectrum matters, coordination and:

(1) Provides oversight, policy and guidance.

(2) Provides primary membership for the department to the IRAC.

(3) Designates alternate members to the IRAC and its subcommittees.

(4) Ensures MCEB participants support DON spectrum policy and interests.

(5) DON national level spectrum management organization is outlined in figure 1-1.

c. <u>Assistant Secretary of the Navy, Research, Development and Acquisition (ASN(RDA))</u>

(1) Establishes policy for the development and acquisition S-D equipment and systems.

(2) Ensures DON acquisition instructions address spectrum supportability.

(3) Ensure DON acquisition programs acquiring S-D equipment and systems adhere to Federal, DOD and DON policy, guidance and instructions.

(4) Maintains awareness of emerging technologies for potential adoption.

6. <u>United States Marine Corps (USMC)</u>

a. <u>Commandant of the Marine Corps (CMC)</u>. The CMC is responsible for spectrum use, management, operations and requirements in support of the Marine Corps operating forces (OPFOR), installations, organizations and activities. CMC is responsible for the Marine Corps management of the electromagnetic spectrum and exercises operational authority by providing command structure and resources to ensure spectrum access to the MAGTF.

b. <u>Director, Command, Control, Communications and Computers (C4), Headquarters, U.S. Marine Corps (HQMC)/Department of the Navy (DON) Deputy Chief Information Officer (Marine Corps) (DDCIO(MC))</u>. Director, C4/DDCIO(MC) provides Marine Corps electromagnetic spectrum policy, and oversees spectrum use, requirements and operations.

c. <u>Commander, Marine Corps Systems Command (MARCORSYSCOM)</u>. MARCORSYSCOM, as the research, development, test and evaluation

(RDT&E) and acquisition organization for the Marine Corps, provides spectrum supportability, certification and frequency coordination in support of and during the acquisition process.

d. <u>Commanders, U.S. Marine Corps Forces (MARFOR)</u>. MARFORs provide spectrum policy, oversight and operational support to the Commanders, Marine Expeditionary Forces (MEF), Marine Corps Installations (MCI), Major Subordinate Commands (MSC), and other Marine Corps organizations and activities in support of day-to-day training, exercises and operations, as well as warfighting responsibilities, where required, to the CCDR within their areas of responsibility (AOR).

(1) In order to maintain DON alignment with national level (NTIA) spectrum management processes within US&P, Marine Corps OPFOR, installations, organizations and activities shall coordinate spectrum management operational requirements and support with the Navy Marine Corps Spectrum Center (NMSC), via its regional support activities, Navy and Marine Corps Spectrum Offices (NMCSO). Regional NMCSO areas of responsibility are identified in figure 1-2.

(2) Outside US&P (OUS&P), Marine Corps OPFOR, installations, organizations and activities shall coordinate spectrum management support with their respective regional COCOM or JFC via their respective Marine Corps Service Component (i.e., MARFOR) or Functional Component.

Note: Marine Corps units afloat (e.g., Marine Expeditionary Units (MEUs), etc.) coordinate spectrum management support via the Expeditionary Strike Group (ESG) chain-of-command once they become operationally controlled (OPCON) to the ESG. Once transitioned ashore or reassigned to the JFC, operational spectrum management support shifts to the supported Marine Corps Service Component (i.e., MARFOR) or Functional Component respectively.

7. <u>Navy and Marine Corps Spectrum Center (NMSC)</u>

a. NMSC, a Tier IV command under Naval Network Warfare Command (NETWARCOM), functions as the spectrum supportability and frequency coordination activity for the Navy and Marine Corps and provides administrative, engineering and operational spectrum management support to the Marine Corps OPFOR, installations, organizations and activities. NMSC provides the following support functions to the Marine Corps:

(1) Provides administrative support, engineering analysis and operational advice to the Marine Corps, as required, in support of spectrum policy determinations, development and governance.

(2) Provides Marine Corps representation, as requested, to various international, national, DOD, Joint and Service related spectrum management forums.

(3) Provides engineering expertise, technical guidance and support during the acquisition lifecycle in support of the spectrum supportability and certification process to include:

(a) Technical guidance and advice throughout all phases of the acquisition lifecycle to include requirements development, system development, acquisition and procurement through system sustainment in support of the spectrum supportability process, specifically:

1. Development, submission, tracking, certification and documentation of Application for Equipment Frequency Allocations (DD-1494).

2. Coordination of DD-1494s with the MCEB ESGPWG to include national level coordination for spectrum supportability determination and certification with the NTIA SPS; host nation coordination/host nation approval (HNC/HNA) for spectrum supportability with the respective regional COCOM in support of Marine Corps operational requirements in foreign nations within their AORs; and documentation of spectrum supportability, certification and HNC within the respective national and DOD spectrum management data repositories.

(b) Provides national level coordination, procurement, registration, assignment and protection within US&P of Marine Corps frequency assignments and resources and assists in the maintenance and review of frequency assignment records.

(c) Provides advice in operational matters for the exploitation of the electromagnetic environment (EME) in order to control electromagnetic interference (EMI) degradation to Marine Corps spectrum operations.

(d) Provides engineering and technical support involving EMI events and provide solutions in order to eliminate and mitigate harmful EMI to the Marine Corps OPFOR, installations, organizations and activities.

(e) Coordinates DON radio frequency spectrum requirements for use during national emergencies and ensures adequate documentation within the NTIA's National Emergency Readiness Plan (NERP).

(f) Provides and maintains regional NMCSO within US&P in support of Marine Corps operational spectrum requirements.

b. <u>Navy and Marine Corps Spectrum Office (NMCSO)</u>. NMCSOS' act as regional Frequency Management Offices (FMO) for NMSC and provide administrative and operational spectrum management support to the Marine Corps OPFOR, installations, organizations and activities within US&P. US&P NMCSOS' are located at (see also figure 1-2):

(1) NMCSO Atlantic - Norfolk, Virginia

(2) NMCSO Pacific - Honolulu, Hawaii

(3) NMCSO Southwest - San Diego, California

(4) NMCSO Northwest - Puget Sound, Washington

(5) NMCSO Guam - Guam

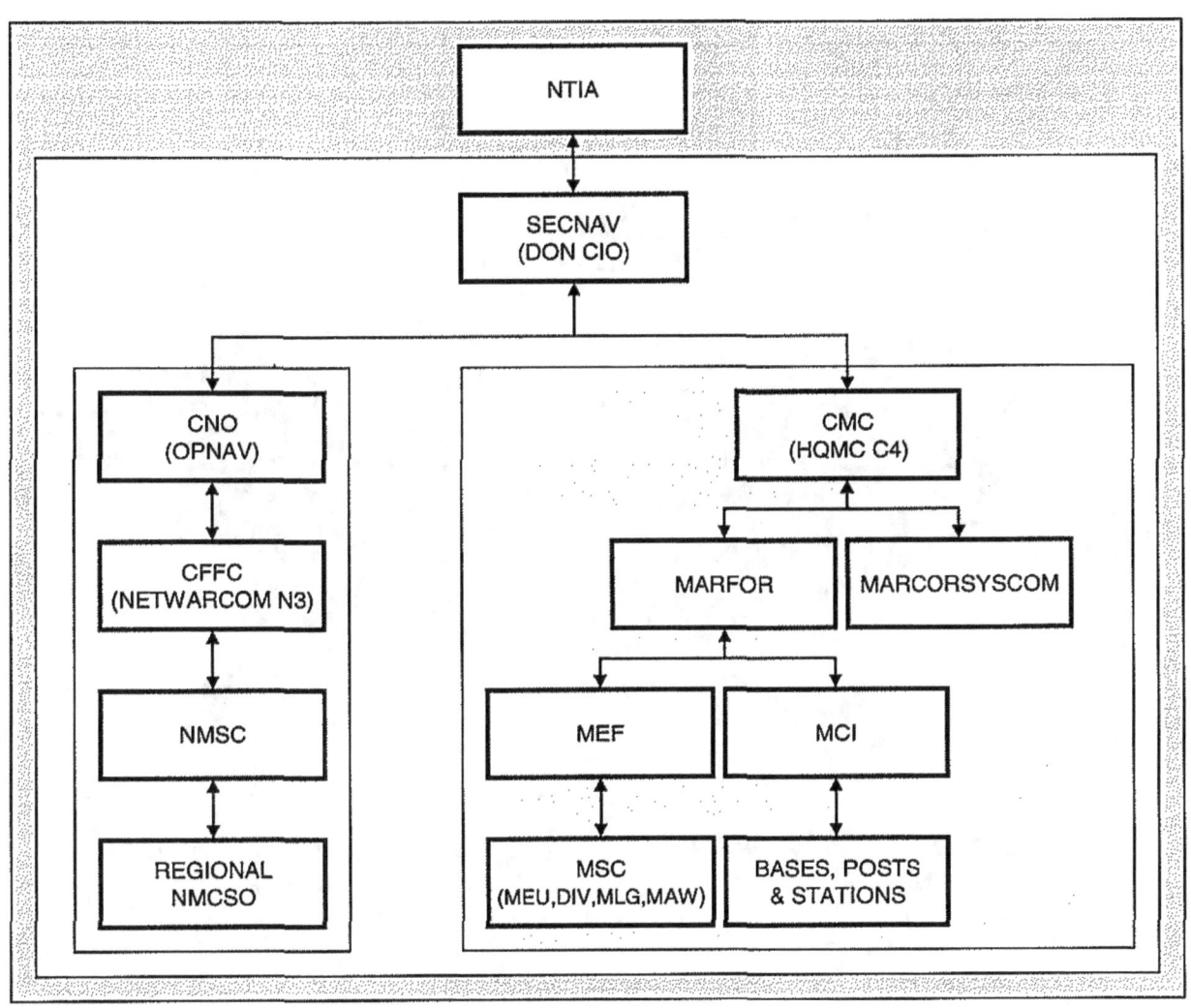

Figure 1-1. --Department of the Navy (DON) National
Level Spectrum Management Organization

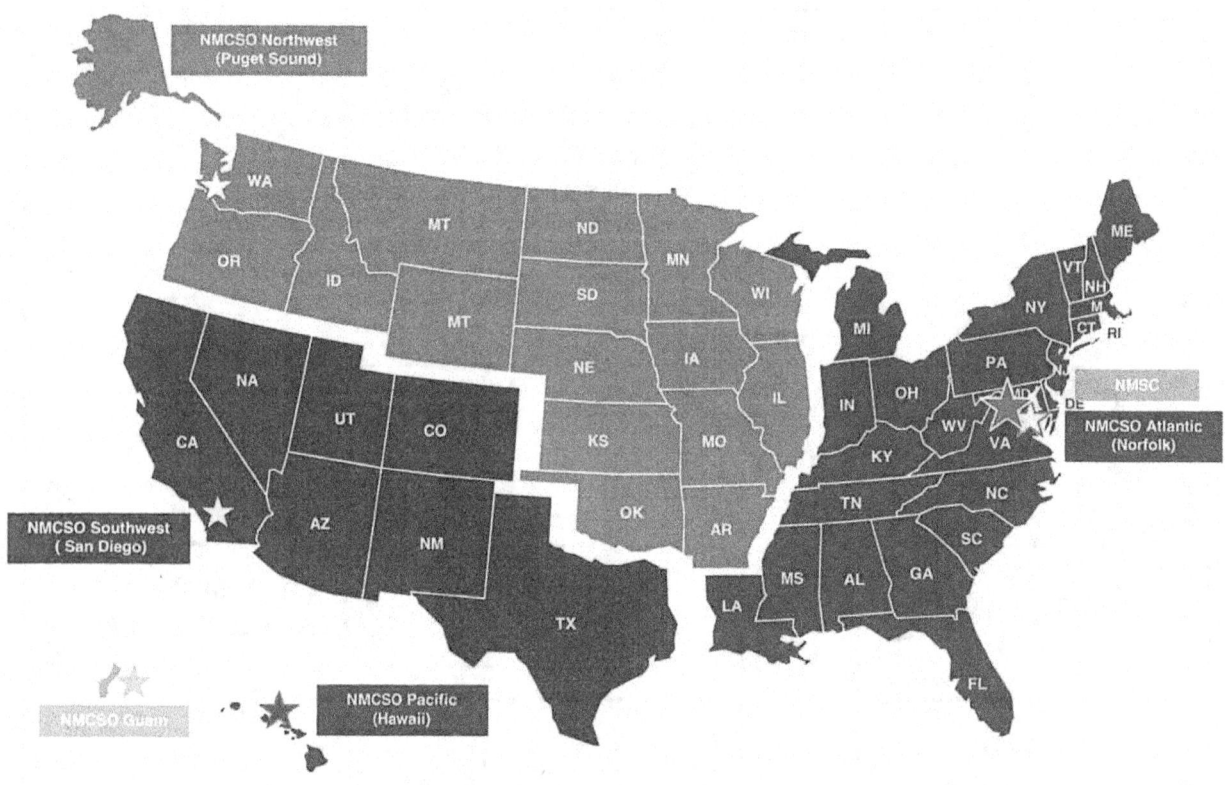

Figure 1-2. --Navy and Marine Corps Spectrum Center (NMSC)
and US&P Regional Navy and Marine Corps Spectrum
Office (NMCSO) Locations

Enclosure (1)

Chapter 2

Spectrum Supportability and Certification

1. Introduction. Spectrum supportability is critical to the Marine Corps ability to comprehend, coordinate and integrate the use of spectrum-dependent (S-D) equipment and systems into the operational electromagnetic environment (EME). The purpose of the spectrum supportability and certification process is to identify and document accurate system characteristics, technical data and administrative information in order to properly, effectively and safely integrate these systems into the critically saturated EME. Spectrum supportability and certification ensures there are sufficient spectrum resources available to support the operational use of the S-D equipment or system. The spectrum supportability and certification process actively supports U.S. national and international spectrum policy concerning the use of the electromagnetic spectrum. Spectrum supportability and certification is the responsibility of the acquisition process and must be considered during all phases of the system lifecycle to include requirements development, system development, acquisition, procurement and system sustainment throughout its operational life.

2. Spectrum Supportability and Certification. In accordance with references (a) through (f), the spectrum supportability and certification process ensures S-D equipment and systems procured by and fielded by the Marine Corps are:

    a. Compliant with international, national, DOD, Joint and Service level statutory and regulatory policy and guidelines for the effective and efficient use of the electromagnetic spectrum.

    b. Ensures S-D equipment and systems fielded by the Marine Corps possess reasonable assurance that sufficient spectrum resources will be available when operationally fielded to the intended user.

    c. Ensures electromagnetic compatibility (EMC) and operational integration are fully considered along with competing S-D equipment and systems within the intended EME.

3. Responsibility for Spectrum Supportability and Certification

    a. Marine Corps Systems Command (MARCORSYSCOM), as the research, development, test and evaluation (RDT&E) and acquisition organization for the Marine Corps, is the focal point for, and is responsible to ensure spectrum supportability and certification are completed during the acquisition process.

b. MARCORSYSCOM ensures a consolidated entry point to the DOD and national level spectrum supportability and certification process for MARCORSYSCOM POs, JPOs where the Marine Corps is the EA, MCWL and procurements by the Marine Corps OPFOR, installations, organizations and activities for spectrum supportability, certification and HNC during the acquisition process. MARCORSYSCOM provides:

(1) Oversight and management of the spectrum supportability and certification process to ensure seamless integration of S-D equipment and systems into the operational EME.

(2) Administrative and technical support to MARCORSYSCOM Program Offices (PO), Joint Program Offices (JPO) where the Marine Corps is the Executive Agent (EA), Marine Corps Warfighting Lab (MCWL) and procurements by the Marine Corps operating forces (OPFOR), installations, organizations and activities for spectrum supportability, certification and host nation coordination (HNC) during the acquisition process.

4. <u>Systems that Require Spectrum Supportability and Certification</u>

a. Spectrum supportability and certification is required for any conceptual, experimental, developmental or operational transmitter, receiver or device (unclassified or classified) that utilizes any portion or part of the electromagnetic spectrum.

b. S-D equipment and systems include, but are not limited to transmitters, receivers, C2 systems and platforms (including satellite communications (SATCOM)), ISR systems and platforms (either manned or unmanned), EW assets, sensors, beacons, navigational aids (NAVAIDS), radar, lasers, munitions and weapons systems.

c. There is no distinction as to the method of procurement to include program and non-program of record; Government developed or Government-off-the shelf (GOTS); Commercial-off-the-shelf (COTS); commercial lease; or operational and maintenance (O&M)/unit funded.

d. Rapid Acquisition (Universal Needs Statement (UNS)/ Urgent-Universal Needs Statement (U-UNS)).

(1) It may be necessary for S-D equipment and systems procured via the rapid acquisition process and to delay spectrum supportability and certification in order to field an emergency or time critical capability to the Marine Corps OPFOR. However, the spectrum supportability and certification process shall be completed as soon as feasibly possible.

(2) Many UNS/U-UNS later become programs of record (POR) or are subsequently fielded to the Marine Corps OPFOR once the technology or concept has proven beneficial. Completion of the spectrum supportability and certification process ensures the intended user can obtain the required spectrum resources once the S-D equipment and systems are fielded to the intended user.

(3) HNC cannot be waived for rapidly acquired S-D equipment and systems. PO and affected commanders must seek HNC support via the regional COCOM or JTF via the respective Functional Component or Marine Corps Service Component. Host nation approval (HNA) must be granted prior to operational use.

5. Spectrum Supportability and Certification Requirements

   a. In accordance with references (a) through (f), the following requirements shall be completed:

   (1) A spectrum supportability determination (i.e., certification) shall be completed in order to provide reasonable assurance that sufficient electromagnetic spectrum resources will be available prior to the S-D equipment or system being operationally fielded to the intended user.

   (2) Spectrum supportability and certification shall be initiated as early as possible and in parallel with other procurement activities during the acquisition process.

       (a) In accordance with reference (e), no S-D equipment or system being developed shall proceed into the System Development and Demonstration Phase without a spectrum supportability determination unless specific authorization to proceed is granted by the Milestone Decision Authority (MDA).

       (b) In accordance with reference (e), no S-D equipment or system shall proceed into the Production and Deployment Phase without such a spectrum supportability determination unless specific authorization to proceed is granted by the Under Secretary of Defense for Acquisition, Technology and Logistics (USD(AT&L) or a waiver granted by the

Assistant Secretary of Defense for Networks and Information
Integration (ASD(NII)).

(3) Spectrum supportability and certification shall be
completed at each the following stages:

(a) <u>Stage 1 (Conceptual)</u>: Stage 1 certification is
intended to provide the PO/PM with regulatory and technical
guidance on the feasibility of obtaining spectrum supportability
and certification during subsequent stages of development.
Stage 1 certification does not support radiation of the S-D
equipment or system. S-D equipment and systems are:

<u>1</u>. Reviewed for conformance against
international and national tables of allocation.

<u>2</u>. Reviewed for conformance against existing
technical standards and sharing criteria.

<u>3</u>. Comparisons are made in regards to known
similar systems and spectrum efficiency is considered.

<u>4</u>. System data will be estimated and only gross
calculations may be achievable for general evaluation and
spectrum impact, which may be subject to adjustment during later
stages of certification.

(b) <u>Stage 2 (Experimental)</u>: Stage 2 certification
is a prerequisite for authorization to radiate in support of
experimentation. Stage 2 certification is intended to provide
analysis of S-D equipment and systems utilizing test equipment,
modified operational equipment, or initial design models that
can be used to determine feasible frequency bands, proposed
equipment configurations or to investigate additional courses of
action in order to obtain certification and spectrum
supportability during subsequent stages of development.
Recommendations for changes to equipment characteristics and
operational employment are provided.

(c) <u>Stage 3 (Developmental)</u>: Stage 3 certification
is required when the major system or subsystem design has been
completed and requires radiation for testing and evaluation. At
Stage 3, the intended frequency band will normally have been
determined and certification at Stage 3 will be required for
testing of proposed operational hardware and potential equipment
configurations. Stage 3 certification requires <u>measured</u> (except
where measured data is not available, then calculated data may

be used) data and provides guidelines for assuring spectrum
supportability at Stage 4.

(d) Stage 4 (Operational): At Stage 4, development
has been essentially completed and final operating constraints
or restrictions required to assure compatibility need to be
identified. Stage 4 certification is required for any S-D
equipment or system with an operational station class (i.e.,
other than experimental). Stage 4 certification requires
measured data and provides operating parameters and restrictions
on the operation of the S-D equipment or system as may be
necessary to prevent harmful electromagnetic interference (EMI).
Following Stage 4 certification, final operating constraints and
restrictions required to assure electromagnetic compatibility
(EMC) have been identified.

(4) S-D equipment and systems procured after a specific
developmental stage need only complete the respective spectrum
supportability stage (e.g., a COTS emitter developed for civil
use, commercially available and purchased by a PO for a tactical
application must complete the certification requirement for
Stage 4 (operational)).

(5) S-D equipment and systems being developed, procured
by and fielded via the Navy acquisition process (e.g., Space and
Naval Warfare Systems Command (SPAWAR), Naval Sea Systems
Command (NAVSEA) and Naval Air Systems Command (NAVAIR) shall
comply with the spectrum supportability and certification
requirements defined in reference (g) and provisions of this
Order.

(6) Prior to acquisition or procurement, S-D equipment
and systems being developed and fielded via the Army, Air Force
or other Federal Government agency's acquisition processes shall
comply with the spectrum supportability and certification
provisions of this Order.

(7) Spectrum supportability and certification support
for DOD organizations without frequency management personnel
(e.g., Defense Information Systems Agency (DISA), Defense
Intelligence Agency (DIA), Defense Advanced Research Projects
Agency (DARPA), etc.), and when the program/project is not
specifically in support of the Marine Corps, shall be provided
by the respective Service level spectrum management agency in
accordance with reference (h). Prior to formal acquisition or
procurement of a S-D equipment or system that has been developed
by one of these organizations, the PO/PM shall ensure spectrum

supportability and certification has been provided for in accordance with the provisions of this Order.

6. Electromagnetic Environmental Effects (E3)

    a. In accordance with references (i) and (j), electromagnetic environmental effects (E3) shall be considered as early as possible during the technology design and development phases of the system and that capabilities and modifications required to minimize and mitigate harmful E3 will be developed and maintained.

    b. All electrical and electronic systems, subsystems and equipment (including ordinance containing electrically initiated devices) shall be mutually compatible in their intended EME without causing or suffering unacceptable mission degradation due to E3.

    c. E3 issues (in regards to operational effectiveness and suitability of Marine Corps weapons, command, control, communications, intelligence, surveillance and information systems) shall be identified and addressed during the four design stages and prior to entering the systems demonstration, production and deployment phases. At a minimum, the following conditions will be considered, addressed and documented:

        (1) Hazards of Electromagnetic Radiation to Ordinance (HERO).

        (2) Hazards of Electromagnetic Radiation to Personnel (HERP).

        (3) Hazards of Electromagnetic Radiation to Fuel (HERF).

7. Host Nation Coordination (HNC)/Host Nation Authorization (HNA). All S-D equipment and systems developed and procured have the potential to be forward deployed by the Marine Corps OPFOR or installed aboard Marine Corps installations overseas. HNC/HNA shall be completed for all S-D equipment or systems prior to being operationally fielded to the intended user outside US&P (OUS&P).

    a. Spectrum supportability and operational use of S-D equipment and systems in a foreign country is authorized only at the behest of the "sovereign" host nation. Marine Corps OPFOR, installations, organizations and activities have no vested or recognized right of access to the electromagnetic spectrum without HNA. In some cases, spectrum supportability may not be feasible and frequency support may not be granted. The host nation has the right to restrict, revoke or deny Marine Corps access to the electromagnetic spectrum at any time, with or without reason/cause.

    b. HNC/HNA is coordinated with the host nation by the regional COCOM and documented by the Military Communications-Electronics Board (MCEB) Equipment Spectrum Guidance Permanent Working Group (ESGPWG).

        (1) Marine Corps organizations and activities shall not coordinate directly with any host nation for spectrum supportability or frequency support.

        (2) Marine Corps Service Components shall coordinate all operational HNC/HNA spectrum supportability issues with their respective regional COCOM's Joint Frequency Management Office (JFMO) or Joint Task Force (JTF) Joint Spectrum Management Element (JSME). Parallel coordination with MARCORSYSCOM and NMSC is required to ensure host nation comments and certification documentation is captured and updated within the respective equipment certification databases for future use.

        (3) Coordination and completion of HNA is critical prior to the fielding of S-D equipment and systems to the Marine Corps OPFOR, installations, organizations or activities OUS&P. Lack of proper and timely HNC/HNA may cause significant delays during the fielding of a S-D equipment and/or system. Examples are, but not limited to:

            (a) Additional host nation requests or clarification of technical or engineering data for proper deconfliction within the EME and/or the host nation's national allocation tables.

            (b) The requested S-D equipment or system is not supportable within the intended EME (e.g., operational frequency bands interfere with safety of life or flight systems, etc.)

        (4) HNC requests for new S-D equipment and systems will be coordinated with all potential foreign nations where the Marine Corps may regularly or potentially operate. MARCORSYSCOM shall maintain a validated list of host nations and HNC requirements, by COCOM AOR, for coordination during the spectrum supportability and certification process.

            (a) HNC requests for new S-D equipment and systems will be submitted to all regional COCOMs for HNC/HNA within their respective AORs.

(b) HNC requests for previously fielded S-D equipment and systems (i.e., those that require an additional HNA than is on the current certification) will be audited upon receipt. Any additional or missing locations shall be added to the request to be coordinated with the COCOM via the ESGPWG. This ensures certifications are being updated in accordance with operational requirements.

(5) Once approved, MARCORSYSCOM shall ensure that HNA comments are updated within the certification documentation and within the appropriate certification databases.

(6) The approval of a J/F 12 certification does not constitute an authority to operate. An authorized frequency assignment must be requested and coordinated with a cognizant frequency assignment authority in accordance with Chapter 3 of this enclosure.

8. <u>Spectrum Supportability and Certification Process</u>

a. The spectrum supportability and certification process starts with the completion and submission of an Application for Equipment Frequency Allocation DD Form 1494 (DD-1494). The spectrum supportability and certification process is outlined in figure 2-1.

b. There are three types of certification actions:

(1) <u>New Application</u>

(a) A DD-1494 is required for any new S-D equipment or system that does not posses an existing certification (J/F 12 number).

(b) The DD-1494 identifies, captures and documents the S-D equipment or system's characteristics, technical data and administrative information.

(c) Once approved, the DD-1494 submission is assigned a "J/F 12" certification number and input into the Spectrum Certification System (SCS) database for DOD wide visibility.

(d) POs are responsible for and shall coordinate with vendors/manufacturers to ensure S-D equipment and system data within the DD-1494 is complete, and accurate as possible during the spectrum certification process.

(2) <u>Modification to an Existing Application</u>

(a) A modification to an existing certification is required when there is any technical modification to an existing J/F 12 certification.

(b) The DD-1494 is used to identify, capture and document the modification of the S-D equipment or system's technical parameters to ensure the J/F 12 certification is updated.

(c) Once approved, the modification DD-1494 is assigned a "slash" designator to the J/F 12 and input into the SCS database for DOD wide visibility.

(d) POs are responsible for and shall coordinate with vendors/manufacturers, to ensure S-D equipment and system data within the DD-1494 is complete, and accurate as possible during the spectrum certification process.

(3) <u>Note-to-Holder (NTH)</u>

(a) A NTH request is required for any administrative modification to an existing J/F 12 certification. Administrative modifications may include, but are not limited to:

<u>1</u>. The addition of another Service to an existing approved J/F 12 certification coordinated by another Service or organization.

<u>2</u>. Modifications or additions to a system's nomenclature.

<u>3</u>. Addition, deletion or changes to approved operating locations.

<u>4</u>. Requests for additional HNC.

<u>5</u>. Modification or change of manufacturer information.

(b) NTH requests shall be submitted to MARCORSYSCOM for coordination with NMSC and NTIA.

(c) Marine Corps OPFOR, installations, organizations and activities requiring NTH action shall submit requests to MARCORSYSCOM, via the respective MARFOR, for coordination with

NMSC and NTIA. Once approved, NTH are added to the J/F 12 documentation and input into the SCS database for DOD wide visibility.

(d) NTH requests requiring HNC/HNA action shall be coordinated with the regional COCOM, via the ESGPWG. Once approved, the foreign nation responses are added to the J/F 12 documentation and input into the Host Nation Spectrum World-wide Database Online (HNSWDO) for DOD wide visibility.

c. Submission Procedures

(1) All spectrum supportability and certification packages and NTH shall be submitted to MARCORSYSCOM for review, submission and tracking.

(a) New submission, modification or NTH packages from POs, JPOs and MCWL shall be submitted directly to MARCORSYSCOM for processing.

(b) New submission, modification or NTH packages from the Marine Corps OPFOR, installations, organizations or activities shall be submitted to MARCORSYSCOM, via the respective MARFOR.

(2) Upon receipt, MARCORSYSCOM will conduct a comprehensive review for administrative correctness, adequacy of technical data and required supporting documentation. The following supporting documentation is required:

(a) New Submission and Modification Packages

1. An application for Equipment Frequency Allocation (DD-1494) shall be completed to include:

a. DOD General Information page.

b. Transmitter Equipment Characteristics page.

c. Receiver Equipment Characteristics page.

d. Antenna Equipment Characteristic page.

e. NTIA General Information page.

<u>2</u>. Request for HNC

<u>a</u>. Foreign Coordination General page.

<u>b</u>. HNC request and country list enclosure.

<u>c</u>. Foreign Disclosure letter.

(b) <u>NTH Submission Packages</u>. Original request for NTH - required endorsements.

(3) <u>Classification of DD-1494</u>

(a) DD-1494s and J/F 12s shall be classified based upon operational requirements and in accordance with reference (k) as well as any other applicable program or system classification guidance. Submitters should ensure DD-1494 or NTH are not unnecessarily classified.

(b) Classified DD-1494s and J/F 12s will contain the appropriate declassification instructions.

(4) <u>Foreign Disclosure</u>. In accordance with reference (h), requests for HNC/HNA shall possess a foreign disclosure statement issued by a Principle Designated Disclosure Authority (PDA) or Designated Disclosure Authority (DDA) to ensure sensitive or classified information on S-D equipment or systems is not inappropriately released to a foreign nation or entity. Foreign disclosure statements should indicate whether all or only specific portions of the technical data is releasable to a specific host nation.

d. <u>Records Management</u>

(1) All spectrum supportability, certification, documentation, approvals and authorizations (e.g., DD-1494, J/F 12, NTH, HNC/HNA, etc.) shall be maintained in accordance with reference (y) (SSIC 3900.1(b) and (2) and SSIC 2410.1-2).

(2) All E3 and EMC analysis and documentation shall be maintained in accordance with reference (y) (SSIC 2450.1-5).

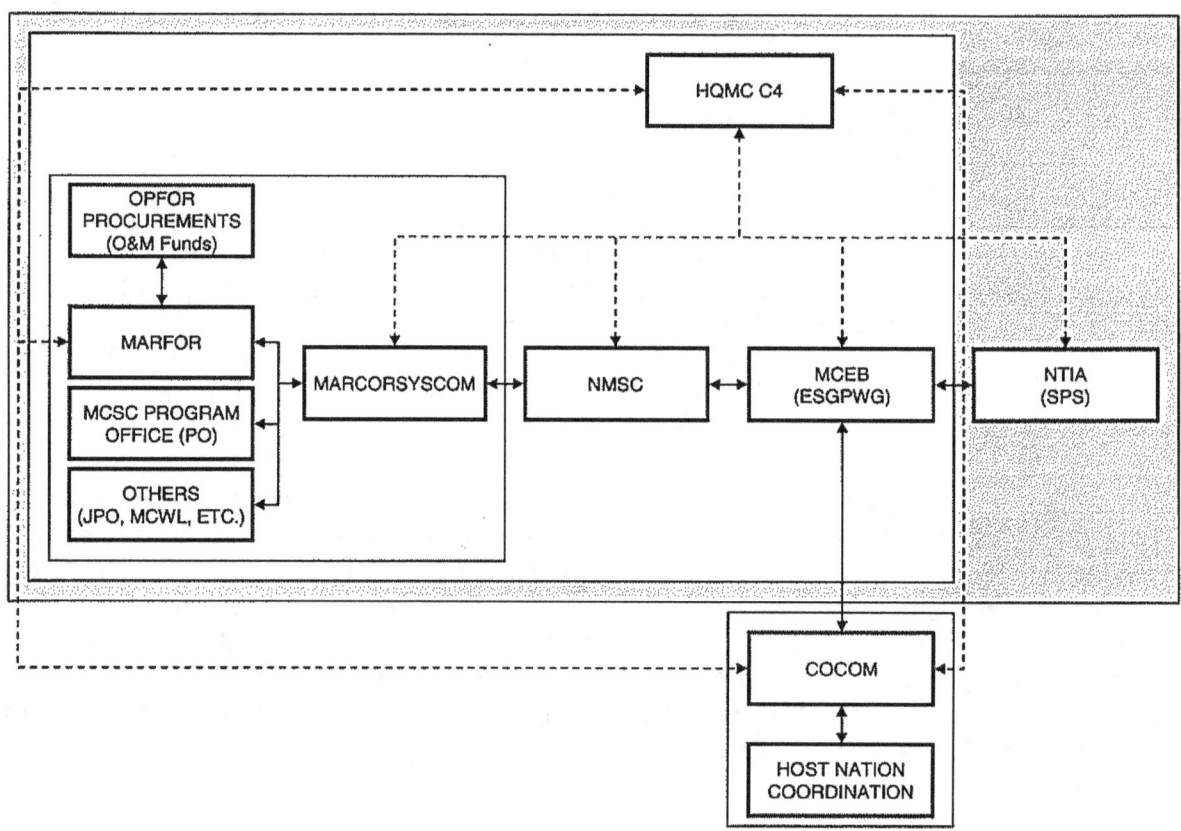

Figure 2-1. --Spectrum Supportability and
Certification Process

Chapter 3

Spectrum Management Operations

1. Introduction. The purpose of this chapter is to provide
policy, guidance, standardization and continuity of operations
to the Marine Corps Operating Forces (OPFOR), installations,
organizations and activities in support of the spectrum
management operational requirements.

2. Spectrum Management Automated Tools and Databases

    a. Spectrum XXI (SXXI)

        (1) SXXI is a client/server, Windows-based software
system that provides a single information system that addresses
spectrum management automation requirements. SXXI supports
operational planning as well as near real-time management of
radio frequency spectrum with an emphasis on assigning
compatible frequencies and performing spectrum engineering
tasks. Interconnected through a Wide Area Network (WAN), the
software extends connectivity to civilian, military and Federal
spectrum management entities.

        (2) In accordance with reference (1), SXXI is designated
as the "Joint Standard" frequency assignment system and will be
used by all Marine Corps OPFOR, installations, organizations and
activities for managing frequency assignment records,
coordination and submission of frequency proposals and perform
interference analysis. Normally, Marine Corps SXXI clients
reside at the installation, Marine Division (MARDIV), Marine
Logistics Group (MLG) or Marine Air Wing (MAW) levels and above.
Subordinate elements requiring spectrum management support
should request assistance via their chain-of-command.

        (3) Access to the SXXI database is restricted. Requests
for access should be submitted to the Joint Spectrum Center
(JSC).

              SXXI Help-desk
              COMM   (410) 293-7994
              DSN   (312) 281-7994
              NIPRNET   SXXIhelp@disa.mil
              SIPRNET   SXXIhelp@disa.smil.mil

b. <u>Government Master File (GMF)</u>

(1) The GMF contains records of frequency assignments for all U.S. Government agencies in the United States and Possessions (US&P).

(2) GMF data is updated into the SXXI database daily to reflect those frequency assignment actions agreed upon by the NTIA Frequency Assignment Subcommittee (FAS). In most cases, Marine Corps activities will not require access to the GMF.

(3) Requests for GMF distribution may be submitted to NTIA via the agency's IRAC representative. Marine Corps activities may request GMF distribution or requests for address changes by contacting HQMC C4:

```
COMM      (703) 693-3477
DSN       (312) 223-3477
NIPRNET   HQMC_C4_SPECTRUM@usmc.mil
SIPRNET   HQMC_C4_SPECTRUM@hqmc.usmc.smil.mil
```

c. <u>Spectrum Certification System (SCS)</u>

(1) The SCS is an automated system used in the preparation of Applications for Equipment Frequency Allocation (DD-1494); for submission of DD-1494 applications into the spectrum supportability process; and is a data repository for certified S-D equipment and systems and their associated technical data once an approved certification (J/F 12 number) has been assigned. SCS serves as the primary data source for technical information on S-D equipment and systems used to support the coordination of operational frequency assignments.

(2) Access to the SCS is restricted by security classification and due to inclusion of proprietary technical data and information included in the database. Industry vendors and contractors must submit requests for SCS data and certification information to MARCORSYSCOM, via their respective Program Office (PO). Marine Corps OPFOR, installations, organizations and activities may request SCS distribution by the JSC:

```
Joint Spectrum Center (JSC)
COMM      (410) 293-2282
DSN       (312) 281-2282
NIPRNET   jscdatabaseowner@disa.mil
```

d. Host Nation Spectrum Worldwide Database Online (HNSWDO)

(1) HNSWDO is a web application that facilitates warfighter deployment and communications by providing worldwide visibility of host nation radio frequency (RF) S-D equipment supportability. HNSWDO automates distribution of host nation coordination requests and COCOM submissions of host nation supportability comments, reducing the time required to manage the process.

(2) HNSWDO enables spectrum managers to determine historical supportability of similar systems' radio frequency (RF) spectrum. This enables informed design decision-making concerning frequency bands, thereby mitigating the risk of acquiring potentially unsupportable RF dependant systems.

(3) HNSWDO maintains a classified and unclassified database. Access to the HNSWDO database is restricted. Requests for access should be submitted to the Joint Spectrum Center (JSC).

```
HNSWDO Help-desk
COMM        (410) 293-9760
DSN         (312) 281-9760
NIPRNET     HNSWDO@disa.mil
SIPRNET     HNSWDOhelpdesk@disa.smil.mil
```

e. JSC Database Access Web-server (JDAWS)

(1) JDAWS is hosted and maintained by the JSC and provides access to the JSC spectrum databases and reports. JDAWS contains data and correspondence for:

(a) Equipment characteristics (tactical and space) derived from the Joint Equipment Tactical and Space (JETS) database.

(b) Electronic Order of Battle (EOB) Data.

(c) Spectrum Certification System (SCS) and J/F 12 Archive.

(d) Frequency usage data.

(e) Country emitter studies.

(f) Interference Incident Reports.

(g) Data Modeling Capabilities.

(2) Access to JDAWS is restricted. Requests for access should be submitted to the Joint Spectrum Center (JSC).

```
JDAWS Help-desk
COMM        (410) 293-2630
DSN         (312) 281-2630
SIPRNET     jdaws@disa.smil.mil
```

f. <u>Systems Planning, Engineering and Evaluation Device (SPEED)</u>

(1) SPEED is a modular communications engineering and analysis tool, which provides planners the ability to rapidly perform a wide range of communications planning, RF engineering and spectrum management functionality. Spectrum managers use SPEED to coordinate and deconflict S-D equipment and systems during all phases of MAGTF operational planning. SPEED features:

(a) Point-to-point analysis.

(b) Radio coverage analysis.

(c) Satellite communications planner.

(d) High frequency (HF) communications planner.

(e) Interference and deconfliction analysis.

(f) C2PC track interface.

(g) Radio guard chart.

(h) Table of equipment manager.

(i) Force structure manager.

(j) EPLRS planner.

(k) Spectrum management.

(l) Comm-on-the-move planner.

(m) Land mobile radio planner.

(n) Robust, standard National Geospatial-Intelligence Agency (NGIA) mapping products (i.e., Digital Terrain Elevation Data (DTED level 1 and 2), ARC Digitized Raster Graphics (ADRG), Compressed ARC Digitized Raster Graphics (CADRG), Controlled Image Base (CIB), and Shuttle Radar Topography Mission data (SRTM) (DTED level 1 and 2)).

(2) Marine Corps activities may request/obtain SPEED software and technical support via the MARCORSYSCOM C4I Support Center at Marine Corps Tactical Systems Support Activity (MCTSSA).

Toll Free	1-800-808-7634
COMM	(760) 725-0533
DSN	(312) 365-0533
NIPRNET	mctssasmbc4iscenter@usmc.mil
SIPRNET	c4isupportcenter@mctssa.usmc.smil.mil
MCTSSA Knowledgebase	www.mctssa.usmc.smil.mil

g. Afloat Electromagnetic Spectrum Operations Program (AESOP)

(1) AESOP is the U.S. Navy's software/engineering tool for Strike Group radar and communications planning for coordinating spectrum interoperability in afloat operations. AESOP enables electronic systems to perform their intended functions within the electromagnetic environment without causing or suffering unacceptable EMI. AESOP provides communications planners the ability to plan for, coordinate and properly manage the electromagnetic spectrum through operational, engineering and administrative procedures. AESOP features:

(a) Integrated spectrum planning and deconfliction toolsets.

(b) Model-based EMI analyses of radar, communications, navigational aids (NAVAIDS) and electronic warfare (EW).

(c) Optimization of spectrum use through assignment generation via generic algorithms. Mitigation calculations include adherence to national/international laws, treaties and host nation agreements regarding spectrum use.

(d) Provides visualization of spectrum usage, EMI, net connectivity and radar coverage/detection range.

(e) Platform movement in the electromagnetic environment: waypoints and man-on-the-move.

(f) SATCOM availability analyst and high frequency (HF) propagation analysis.

(g) Provides an automated method of drafting the Operational Tasking Communication (OPTASKCOM) message, which is the means used by allied navies to distribute afloat communications plans.

(2) AESOP is used by all U.S. Navy ships, U.S. Coast Guard vessels, numbered fleet commands and shore commands. Marine Corps activities may request/obtain AESOP software and support via the AESOP help-desk.

```
AESOP Help-desk
COMM      (540) 653-8021
DSN       (312) 249-8021
NIPRNET   aesop@navy.mil
SIPRNET   aesop@navy.smil.mil
```

h. Joint Automated CEOI System (JACS)

(1) JACS is the interface between spectrum managers and communications planners in order to allow for the automated transfer of spectrum management information. JACS is used to create/generate the Communications-Electronics Operations Instruction (CEOI), a directory of C2 nets consisting of assigned radio frequencies and radio call signs/words for use by the warfighter. The CEOI includes challenge and passwords, instructions for coordination of visual communication, SINCGARS hop-set generation and provides specified and unique coordination documents (e.g., Air Tasking Order (ATO) or OPTASKCOM).

(2) JACS provides automated exchange with SXXI for deconfliction of frequency resources and provides outputs to CEOI, ATO and/or OPTASKCOM message formats.

(3) In accordance with references (m) and (n), JACS is designated as the "Joint Standard" CEOI generation tool and will be used by all Marine Corps activities for identification and coordination of applicable tactical nets and circuit requirements; development of the Master Net List (MNL); frequency resource determination; and deconfliction of call sign/words.

(4) Marine Corps activities may request/obtain JACS software and support via the ACES/CT3 help-desk.

> ACES/CT3 Help-desk
> Toll Free 1-866-651-1199
> NIPRNET   acesct3helpdesk@css-inc.biz
> Webpage   https://rdit.army.mil/commsc/menu.cfm

3. Frequency Records and Database Management

a. In accordance with reference (1), SXXI is designated as the "Joint Standard" frequency assignment system and will be used by all Marine Corps OPFOR, installations, organizations and activities for managing frequency assignment records, coordination and submission of frequency proposals and performance of interference analysis.

b. SXXI Job Account Creation and Maintenance. SXXI job accounts are used to distinctly differentiate spectrum management areas of responsibility (AOR). Job accounts are similar to e-mail addresses and provide permissions to the assigned organization. Job accounts are tied to frequency records, statuses, etc. as proposals transit the frequency assignment, approval and review process. Job accounts are assigned to a frequency proposal from creation through approval or deletion from the SXXI database.

(1) Job accounts are established and maintained by Marine Corps OPFOR, installations, organizations and activities requiring access to the SXXI database. Normally, Marine Corps SXXI clients reside at the installation, MARDIV, MLG or MAW levels and above. Subordinate elements requiring spectrum management support should request assistance via their chain-of-command.

(2) Job accounts are considered "organizational accounts" and shall not be created for individual use.

(3) To ensure Marine Corps standardization of job accounts within the SXXI database, job account naming conventions will be in accordance with figure 3-1.

(a) Although not recommended, organizations may create and maintain more than one job account to support short-term operational requirements. However, Marine Corps OPFOR, installations, organizations and activities shall maintain their primary account in accordance with figure 3-1.

(b) Job account administrators shall ensure they are not duplicating an existing account prior to creating additional accounts.

(c) Unused job accounts will be deleted from the SXXI database as soon as no longer required. Job account administrators requiring this action shall contact/coordinate with the SXXI Help-desk.

(d) SXXI job account administrators will ensure point of contact information for their respective Job accounts are up-to-date to include:

    <u>1</u>. Rank/Name.

    <u>2</u>. Organization.

    <u>3</u>. DSN Phone number.

    <u>4</u>. Unclassified e-mail address.

c. <u>Classification of Frequency Records</u>

(1) The aggregated classification of the SXXI database is SECRET.

(2) Frequency records shall be classified based upon operational requirements and in accordance with references (o) and (p). Submitters should ensure frequency proposals/records are not unnecessarily classified.

(a) Within US&P, most frequency records will be assigned a "UE" security classification (UNCLASSIFIED - Not releasable outside the U.S. Government).

(b) Outside US&P, classification of frequency records will be in accordance with established regional COCOM or JTF policy and guidance.

(c) Classified frequency records will contain the appropriate declassification instructions in accordance with references (o) and (p).

d. <u>Marine Corps Agency Serial Numbers</u>

(1) In accordance with reference (c), agency serial numbers are used to identify the organization responsible for maintaining a frequency record and used to track and manage

frequency proposals and assignments within the SXXI database and GMF. Agency serial numbers are assigned by the frequency proposal originator and remains with the proposal/assignment for the duration of the requirement or expiration of the record.

(a) All Marine Corps frequency assignments coordinated with and received from NTIA are procured under the authority and responsibility of the SECNAV, via the DON CIO. Marine Corps administered frequency assignments are identified by the following prefixes:

(b) A "MC" prefix delineates a Marine Corps permanent or temporary assignment (Example: MC 080100).

(c) A "MCT" prefix delineates a Marine Corps Special Temporary Assignment (STA)(Example: MCT 080100).

(2) Within US&P, HQMC C4 provides oversight and coordination of Marine Corps agency serial number blocks in support of the frequency assignment process. III MEF units will comply where Major Subordinate Commands (MSCs) are physically located, operating or training within US&P (e.g., Hawaii, Guam, etc.)

(3) Agency serial number blocks will be assigned and disseminated annually based upon assessment of past usage and future operational spectrum requirements. HQMC C4 will disseminate serial number blocks, by separate correspondence, no later than 1 December of the preceding year in which they will take effect (e.g., MC/MCT serial number blocks for CY-2010 will be assigned no later than 1 Dec 2009).

(a) The following Marine Corps activities will receive agency serial blocks:

<u>1</u>. HQMC C4.

<u>2</u>. MARFORCOM.

<u>3</u>. MARFORPAC.

<u>4</u>. MARSOC.

<u>5</u>. MARFORRES.

<u>6</u>. Other organizations as required.

(b) Receiving organizations may further delegate and sub-assign allotted serial number blocks to their respective MEFs, MCIs, and other subordinate organizations as required. Receiving organizations will provide HQMC C4 documentation of serial number block sub-assignments no later than 30 days after receipt.

(4) Outside US&P, serial number blocks are assigned and usage managed in accordance with established regional COCOM or JTF policy and guidance.

(5) Serial number block assignments and sub-assignments shall be maintained in accordance with reference (y) (SSIC 2400.1).

e. Organizational Information (SFAF 200 Series Data Items)

(1) In accordance with reference (p), SFAF 200 series data items (200-209) serve two purposes:

(a) Identification of the frequency management organizational chain responsible for managing the frequency assignment and the organizations having an area of interest in the assignment area.

(b) Selection and distribution of records. These data items are especially important when assignments are needed promptly in order to meet mission requirements.

(2) Each frequency assignment has a designated management chain. When logically and consistently entered into the assignment record, the data can/will ensure effective management of Marine Corps frequency assignments and records.

(3) In order to standardize the SFAF 200 series data items (200-209) and ensure consistency of data entries, Marine Corps OPFOR, installations, organizations and activities shall use the standardized inputs within figure 3-1, figure 3-2 and in accordance with reference (p).

f. Marine Corps Frequency Record Review Program

(1) Marine Corps OPFOR, installations, organizations and activities have a vested interest in the sustainment and maintenance of frequency record information and emitter data within the SXXI database, GMF and other spectrum management databases. Obsolete or erroneous information directly affects the overall integrity of the database and may significantly

impact the Marine Corps ability to gain access to the electromagnetic spectrum. Proactive database management enables:

(a) Effective engineering analysis, deconfliction, nomination, coordination and interference analysis of electromagnetic spectrum resources within the EME.

(b) Visibility of frequency assignment records for nomination, submission, registration and protection of Marine Corps spectrum resources.

(c) Statistical analysis and spectrum supportability determinations regarding allocation tables and channeling plans in support international, national and DOD spectrum policy.

(d) Planning, coordination and procurement of funding for spectrum resources in support of Marine Corps training, exercises and operations. All Federal Government agencies to include DOD, are assessed monetary fees by NTIA based on annual spectrum usage. In FY-2008, Marine Corps spectrum fees exceeded $600,000 in support of training exercises and operations within US&P and is expected to increase at a steady rate into the foreseeable future.

(2) In accordance with reference (c), the Marine Corps shall establish and maintain a frequency record review program to ensure Marine Corps frequency assignment records are:

(a) Currently in use by the owning organization and to provide updates, modifications or deletions as required.

(b) Validated operational requirements being used for their stated/intended purpose.

(c) Ensure frequency assignments continue to meet the requirements of associated allocation tables, channeling plans and other regulations.

(3) In accordance with references (c) and (p), the following procedures are provided:

(a) Annually, HQMC C4 shall disseminate a consolidated list, broken down by MARFOR, of US&P frequency assignments/records that are currently overdue or that will expire on or before 31 December of the affected year.

<u>1</u>. Consolidated lists will be disseminated no later than 31 January of the affected year.

<u>2</u>. MARFORs shall coordinate with their respective Marine Corps OPFOR, installations, organizations and activities to review, modify or delete the identified frequency assignments/records.

<u>3</u>. MARFORs shall submit a consolidated list of completed/pending actions to HQMC C4 no later than 31 July of the affected year.

(b) The intent of this process is to align the validation and coordination of Marine Corps frequency assignments with the NTIA assessment of spectrum fees. During the review process, the owning unit will complete an overall validation of the operational requirement and make the following determinations:

<u>1</u>. Validation of the operational requirement for continued maintenance of the frequency assignment/record (e.g., the S-D equipment or system is still in the inventory, etc.).

<u>2</u>. Validation of the frequency assignment/ record against applicable frequency allocation tables and channeling plans.

<u>3</u>. Verification and update organizational data (SFAF 200 series data items) in accordance with this chapter and in accordance figure 3-1 and figure 3-2.

<u>4</u>. Verification of emitter data to include:

<u>a</u>. Transmitter data (SFAF 300 series data items) and equipment locations. S-D equipment and systems installed in "fixed" locations (e.g., base stations, repeaters, radar, NAVAIDs, etc.) shall possess actual GPS location entered in the frequency record. Mobile S-D equipment and systems shall include validated operating radius.

<u>b</u>. Receiver data (SFAF 400 series data items) and equipment locations. S-D equipment and systems installed in "fixed" locations (e.g., base stations, repeaters, radar, NAVAIDs, etc.) shall posses actual GPS location entered in the frequency record. Mobile S-D equipment and systems shall include validated operating radius.

c. Certification data (J/F 12).

d. Verify and update requirement description and justification comments.

e. Coordinate with respective regional and area frequency coordinators or other entities as required.

f. Verify and update point of contact information.

(c) Compliance checks shall be run on all frequency proposals prior to submission.

1. Every effort shall be made to validate and correct any identified errors before selecting the "override error" function and submitting the proposal.

2. Frequency proposals submitted without a compliance check or that possess compliance errors not properly mitigated may be returned to the submitter for further action.

(d) Frequency assignments no longer in use/required shall be submitted as "delete" proposals. When deleting frequency assignments, every effort shall be taken to notify all affected users to ensure transmission on invalidated frequency assignments and harmful EMI is avoided.

(e) Due to processing/coordination timelines, modification proposals should be submitted in sufficient time to reach NMSC no later than 30 to 60 days prior to the expiration date of the frequency assignment/record.

(4) Failure to properly review frequency assignments/ records or take appropriate action in a timely manner may result in deletion of frequency assignments/records from the SXXI and GMF databases. Marine Corps OPFOR, installations, organizations and activities who allow operational frequencies to expire relinquish any and all authority to operate.

(5) Frequency assignments/records shall be maintained in accordance with reference (y) (SSIC 2410.2a(1)).

4. Frequency Assignment Process

a. In accordance with reference (c), Marine Corps OPFOR, installations, organizations and activities shall not operate or radiate any S-D equipment or system without first obtaining spectrum supportability/certification and an authorized frequency assignment.

     (1) Possession of an authorized frequency assignment ensures:

        (a) The S-D equipment or system has met the required spectrum supportability and certification requirements.

        (b) Sufficient engineering and analysis has been completed to ensure it will not cause harmful EMI to other authorized users in the band.

        (c) Constitutes authority to operate within the parameters (and in some cases, restrictions) of the frequency assignment.

     (2) The willful, repeated and unauthorized use of S-D equipment or systems that cause harmful EMI to authorized users are subject to Federal actions, which provide for criminal penalties and fines in accordance with reference (q).

     (3) Commanders shall make every effort to ensure compliance.

   b. Frequency assignments will be submitted in accordance with references (c) and (p).

     (1) In accordance with reference (1), SXXI is designated as the "Joint Standard" frequency assignment system and will be used by all Marine Corps OPFOR, installations, organizations and activities for managing frequency assignment, coordination and submission of frequency proposals, and perform interference analysis.

        (a) Marine Corps OPFOR, installations, organizations and activities without SXXI access shall coordinate and submit frequency requests via their respective MARFOR, MEF or MCI chain-of-command.

        (b) Frequency requests shall be submitted in Standard Frequency Action Format (SFAF) in accordance with reference (p).

        (c) Compliance checks shall be run on <u>all</u> frequency proposals prior to submission.

<u>1</u>. Every effort will be made to validate and correct any identified errors before selecting the "override error" function and submitting the proposal.

<u>2</u>. Frequency proposals submitted without a compliance check or that possess compliance errors not properly mitigated may be returned to the submitter for action.

(2) <u>Categories of Frequency Assignments</u>

(a) A Permanent (or Regular) Assignment is a frequency assignment that is valid for an unspecified period of time (minimum of five years). Revalidation and review requirements are subject to the authorization provided when assigned and in accordance with applicable allocation tables and requirements contained in reference (c). Permanent assignments are registered in the GMF.

(b) A Temporary Assignment is a frequency assignment that is valid for not more than five years and possesses an expiration date. Temporary assignments may be reviewed/renewed for additional periods if necessary. Temporary assignments are not registered in the GMF.

(c) A Special Temporary Authorization Assignment (STA) is a short-term temporary authorization for Federal users within US&P. STAs are used to support short duration exercises, events or equipment tests and evaluations. STA assignments may not exceed 180 days. Marine Corps OPFOR, installations, organizations and activities requiring multiple, consecutive STAs in support of operational requirements shall request for a permanent or temporary assignment.

(3) <u>Submission/Coordination Process</u>

(a) In order to maintain DON alignment with national level (NTIA) spectrum management processes within US&P, Marine Corps OPFOR, installations, organizations and activities shall coordinate spectrum management operational requirements and support with the Navy Marine Corps Spectrum Center (NMSC) via its regional support activities, Navy and Marine Corps Spectrum Offices (NMCSO). Regional NMCSO areas of responsibility are identified in figure 1-2. The US&P frequency assignment process is identified in figure 3-4.

<u>1</u>. Additional lateral coordination with other affected agencies and organizations may also be required in support of frequency requests.

<u>2</u>.   Frequency requests should be coordinated with enough lead-time to ensure submissions reach the respective regional NMCSO no later than 30 to 60 days prior to the requested commencement date of operation.   Increased lead-times may be required in support of special systems (e.g., experimental systems, unmanned aerial systems (UAS), IED jammers, etc.).

<u>a</u>.   Contingency operations will be coordinated based upon operational requirements/time frames.

<u>b</u>.   Marine Corps activities should make every effort to plan for spectrum requirements well in advance of required testing, training and exercises to ensure proper national level coordination.

(b) Outside US&P (OUS&P), Marine Corps OPFOR, installations, organizations and activities shall coordinate spectrum management support with their respective regional COCOM or JFC via their respective Marine Corps Service Component (i.e., MARFOR) or Functional Component.   The OUS&P frequency assignment process is identified in figure 3-5.

Note: Marine Corps units afloat (e.g., Marine Expeditionary Units (MEUs), etc.) coordinate spectrum management support via the Expeditionary Strike Group (ESG) chain-of-command once they become operationally controlled (OPCON) to the ESG.   Once transitioned ashore or reassigned to the JFC, operational spectrum management support shifts to the supported Marine Corps Service Component (i.e., MARFOR) or Functional Component respectively.

<u>1</u>.   Frequency requests should be coordinated in accordance with policy and guidance set forth by the regional COCOM or JTF.   However, operational statistics show frequency requests should reach the respective regional COCOM or JTF no later than 90 to 120 days prior to the requested commencement date of operation.

<u>a</u>.   Contingency operations will be coordinated based upon operational requirements/time frames.

<u>b</u>.   Marine Corps activities should make every effort to plan for spectrum requirements well in advance of required testing, training and exercises to ensure proper host nation coordination/host nation approval (HNC/HNA).   Increased lead-times may be required in support of special systems (e.g., experimental systems, UAS, Counter RCIED (Remote

Control Improvised Explosive Device) Electronic Warfare (CREW) systems, etc.).

        <u>2</u>. At no time shall a Marine Corps activity directly contact a host nation or foreign government to coordinate spectrum management support.

5. <u>International Distress and Emergency Frequencies</u>. International distress and emergency frequencies (also referred to as "Taboo" frequencies) are friendly frequencies of such importance that they should never be deliberately jammed or interfered with by friendly forces. A list of Taboo frequencies is identified in figure 3-3. Normally, these frequencies include international distress, CEASE BUZZER, or safety and control frequencies. These frequencies are generally long standing. However, they may be time oriented in that as the situation changes, restrictions may be modified or removed. International distress and emergency frequencies will be clearly identified in all Marine Corps CEOIs and associated communications planning documents (i.e., Annex K).

    a. At no time will a Marine Corps OPFOR, installation, organization or activity assign an international distress or emergency frequency for operational or general use.

    b. International distress and emergency frequencies shall not be used for testing, simulated emergency training, operational checks or maintenance functions.

    c. Any operator/station experiencing an emergency may utilize a international distress and emergency frequency within the intended conditions of use and do not require an authorized frequency assignment. If during an emergency, the operator/station is unable to make positive contact using a designated international distress and emergency frequency, the operator/station may use any available means to obtain assistance or help.

6. <u>Electronic Warfare/Electronic Attack (EW/EA)</u>

    a. EW/EA is any military action involving the use of directed energy to control the electromagnetic spectrum or to attack the enemy. Combat operations require coordination and deconfliction between C2, ISR and EW/EA S-D assets to include Blue Force communications, airborne EW/EA platforms and tactical jamming systems (e.g., IED jammers). EW/EA is not authorized within US&P and there are no specific frequency bands specifically allocated for EW/EA. The ability to test, train and exercise EW/EA capabilities are critical to the effective employment of the Marine Corps OPFOR. EW/EA is highly regulated and generally confined to designated military installations and training areas when specifically authorized.

b. Proper EW/EA coordination minimizes the likelihood of harmful EMI to authorized spectrum users. In accordance with reference (s), EW/EA coordination is required when a requester desires to conduct EW/EA in a frequency band where authorized users of primary and secondary spectrum services are assigned. EW/EA coordination applies to:

(1) Marine Corps OPFOR, installations, organizations and activities engaged in testing, training and/or exercises of EW/EA equipment, systems or platforms.

(2) Marine Corps OPFOR, installations, organizations and activities operating S-D equipment or systems that may be subjected to harmful EMI from EW/EA.

(3) Civilian contractors performing EW/EA for DOD or Marine Corps activities. Civilian contractors must be:

(a) Performing EW/EA under a U.S. military contract.

(b) The EW/EA equipment has been contracted by, for or owned by the U.S. Government.

(c) DOD or Marine Corps representatives must be available to assist the contractor in the application of reference (s) and EW/EA clearance approval.

(d) EW/EA clearance must be on file with the DOD or Marine Corps activity administering the contract.

c. EW/EA Request Procedures

(1) The following procedures will be used when requesting EW/EA clearance for testing, training or exercises within US&P:

(a) EW/EA requests will be submitted to the NMSC via the respective MARFOR. EW/EA requests should be coordinated with enough lead-time to ensure submissions reach NMSC no later than 90 days prior to the requested commencement date.

(b) Marine Corps activities should make every effort to plan EW/EA missions well in advance of required testing, training and exercises to ensure proper national level coordination.

(c) EW/EA requests will be transmitted by official message traffic, via the SIPRNET, no matter the classification of the submission.

(d) Classification will be in accordance with reference (k) as well as any other applicable program or system classification guidance.

(e) EW/EA requests will be formatted in accordance with enclosure (d) of reference (s).

(2) The following procedures will be used when requesting EW/EA clearance for testing, training, exercises or operations OUS&P:

(a) EW/EA requests will be submitted to the regional COCOM or JTF via the respective Functional Component or Marine Corps Service Component. EW/EA submission requirements and lead-times will be in accordance with reference (s) and any additional policy and guidance set forth by the regional COCOM or JTF.

(b) Marine Corps activities should make every effort to plan EW/EA missions sufficiently well in advance of required testing, training and exercises to ensure proper national level coordination.

(c) EW/EA requests will be transmitted by official message traffic, via the SIPRNET, no matter the classification of the submission.

(d) Classification will be in accordance with reference (k) as well as any other applicable program or system classification guidance.

(e) EW/EA requests will be formatted in accordance with reference (s).

(f) At no time will a Marine Corps activity directly contact a host nation or foreign government to coordinate EW/EA support.

(3) <u>EW/EA Activity Against Global Positioning System</u> <u>(GPS)</u>

(a) The Joint Staff (JS) is the approval authority for EW/EA missions with potential impact to GPS frequencies, systems or assets. Evaluation and approval/disapproval of EW/EA requests is based on the following considerations:

<u>1</u>. Potential impact to civil GPS users and potential for damage to receiver equipment.

<u>2</u>. Potential impacts to safety of life and flight operations.

<u>3</u>. Potential for compromising classified capabilities.

(b) EW/EA requests for use against GPS radio navigation bands L1 (1575.42 MHz, +/- 12 MHz) and/or L2 (1227.6 MHz, +/- 12 MHz) will be submitted to the Joint Staff via the respective MARFOR and NMSC. EW/EA requests should be coordinated with enough lead-time to ensure submissions reach the Joint Staff no later than 90 days prior to the requested commencement date.

(c) Marine Corps activities should make every effort to plan EW/EA missions sufficiently well in advance of required testing, training and exercises to ensure proper national level coordination.

(d) EA requests will be transmitted by official message traffic, via the SIPRNET, no matter the classification of the submission.

(e) Classification will be in accordance with reference (k) as well as any other applicable program or system classification guidance.

(f) EW/EA requests will be formatted in accordance with reference (s).

(g) JS will provide approval/disapproval determination no later than 10 days prior to requested commencement date.

(4) <u>Chaff Operations</u>. The use of and restrictions for chaff or rope chaff use are in accordance with reference (s).

(5) "CEASE BUZZER" Procedures

    (a) CEASE BUZZER procedures are initiated when immediate suspension of EW/EA activity is required for safety of life or flight reasons; in cases of harmful EMI to authorized users of the electromagnetic spectrum; for operational security (OPSEC) reasons; and at the determination of the EA authorized user.

    (b) EW/EA incident reporting and notification procedures are in accordance with references (t), (u) and (v).

    (c) CEASE BUZZER procedures will be strictly adhered to and complied with by participating Marine Corps activities during EW/EA testing, training, exercises and operations in accordance with enclosure (h) of reference (s). Marine Corps activities will:

        1. Provide current, validated points of contact information to the controlling agency overseeing the EW/EA mission.

        2. EW/EA authorized users will continuously monitor assigned emergency guard channels for the duration of the EW/EA testing, training, exercise or operation.

        3. EW/EA authorized users will cease operations upon controlling agency notification to suspend EW/EA operations.

        4. EW/EA authorized users will not reinstate EW/EA operations without authorization from the controlling agency that the STOP BUZZER suspension has been lifted.

7. Title 47 U.S.C. Non-Licensed Devices

    a. Non-licensed devices are low power emitters approved for "unlicensed" users under the Federal Communications Commission (FCC) regulations. Technology, use and availability of non-licensed devices have expanded with applications in the home, business, commercial industry and even DOD. Examples of non-licensed devices include but are not limited to Wireless Local Area Networks (WLAN) using Wi-Fi technologies; Bluetooth devices; some hand-held radios; cordless telephones; some wireless microphones, headsets and monitoring devices; and even some UAS use non-licensed devices and frequency bands. These devices typically operate in, but are not limited to the 900 MHz, 2.5 and 5 GHz frequency bands. Non-licensed devices may increase the probability of and are highly susceptible to harmful EMI with the potential to degrade the reliability of other S-D equipment and systems in close proximity. However, non-licensed devices may also provide valuable, supplemental and/or expendable communications services where needed.

b. In accordance with reference (c) and (w), Federal Government agencies may purchase "off the shelf" non-licensed devices that conform to Title 47 of the FCC rules and shall bear the appropriate FCC statement of limitations to operations. Operation of non-licensed devices is subject to the following conditions:

(1) Marine Corps OPFOR, installations, organizations and activities operating a non-licensed device have no vested or recognized right to continued use of the device in any part of the radio frequency spectrum. Non-licensed devices may only be operated in compliance with the applicable "Part" (e.g., Part 15, Part 95, etc.) in accordance with reference (w) and as implemented by reference (c).

(2) Non-licensed devices must operate on a Not-to-Interfere Basis (NIB) and may not cause harmful EMI to any other authorized user.

(3) Non-licensed devices must accept any EMI received, including interference that may cause undesired operation or reliability, even if the harmful EMI renders the device unusable.

(4) Changes or modifications (e.g., frequency, power output or antenna) negate the user's authority to operate the S-D equipment or system under the FCC Rules. Spectrum certification and an authorized frequency assignment is required prior to operating any "modified" non-licensed device.

(5) Marine Corps activities operating non-licensed devices that cause harmful EMI to an authorized user shall promptly take steps to eliminate the EMI. Upon notification by cognizant spectrum management personnel that the device is causing interference, the operator of the non-licensed device shall cease all radiation from the device. Operations shall not resume until the conditions causing the EMI are corrected.

(6) Since non-licensed devices operate NIB, in many cases they do not provide sufficient reliability and should not be used in place of more reliable communications means for critical command and control or other operational communications functions. To ensure adequate regulatory protection, Marine Corps activities shall rely only on S-D equipment and systems

with frequency assignments in the GMF as principal radio communication systems for safeguarding human life or property in accordance with reference (c).

c. In accordance with reference (d) and (e), non-licensed devices require spectrum supportability and certification regardless of its non-licensed use. Non-licensed use does not extend outside US&P and requires all S-D equipment and systems to receive favorable Host Nation Approval (HNA) and frequency approval prior to operation in a foreign nation.

d. Commanders should be aware that non-licensed devices (e.g., wireless modems, cordless phones, baby monitors, etc.) which may have been transported outside US&P in a service member's household goods shipments or imported for commercial sale by the Marine Corps Exchange (MCX) are subject to the same HNC/HNA and frequency approval requirements. Local policy should be provided to Marine Corps personnel, family members and other organizations to ensure they are in compliance with the host nation's regulatory guidance and restrictions.

8. <u>Communications-Electronics Operations Instruction/Joint Communications-Electronics Operations Instruction (CEOI/JCEOI)</u>

a. In accordance with references (m) and (n), JACS is designated as the "Joint Standard" CEOI generation tool and will be used by all Marine Corps activities for identification and coordination of applicable tactical nets and circuit requirements; development of the Master Net List (MNL); frequency resource determination; and deconfliction of call sign/words. The CEOI/JCEOI provides:

(1) MNL (Organizational net/circuit structure).

(2) Coordination of frequency use/re-use and sharing plans.

(3) S-D equipment and system types.

(4) Spectrum requirements and restrictions.

(5) Call sign/word and visual communications requirements (e.g., smoke and pyrotechnics).

b. CEOIs are utilized for Marine Corps specific training, exercises and operations. Although tactical use of the CEOI is at the commander's discretion based on operational mission requirements, commanders are encouraged to develop, maintain and utilize contingency Master Net Lists (MNL) to facilitate deliberate and crisis actions planning.

c. JCEOIs are utilized for Joint training, exercises and operations. In accordance with references (m) and (r), JCEOI use shall be in accordance with established COCOM or JTF policy and guidance. Marine Corps OPFOR and Service Components shall develop, maintain and utilize contingency MNL to facilitate deliberate and crisis actions planning.

d. The senior command/organization in charge of the training, exercise or operation is responsible for coordination, distribution and maintenance of the CEOI/JCEOI.

e. Daily Changing Frequencies

   (1) The use of daily changing frequencies during exercises and operations provides an additional layer of operational security (OPSEC) to Marine Corps communications and tactical networks.

      (a) Tactical use of daily changing frequencies is at the commander's discretion based on operational mission requirements and in accordance with established COCOM or JTF policy and guidance.

      (b) Daily changing frequencies should be used for all tactical, secure or unsecure, single-channel voice and data networks. Frequency agile or frequency hopping networks (e.g., SINCGARS) and safety of life nets (e.g., search and rescue (SAR), range control, etc.) are not subject to daily changing frequency requirements.

f. Daily Changing Voice Call Words/Signs

   (1) The use of daily changing voice call words/signs during exercises and operations provides an additional layer of operational security (OPSEC) to Marine Corps tactical voice communications networks.

      (a) Tactical use of daily changing voice call words/signs is at the commander's discretion based on operational mission requirements and in accordance with reference (x) and established COCOM or JTF policy and guidance.

      (b) Daily changing voice call words/signs should be used for all tactical, secure or non-secure, single-channel and frequency hopping voice networks (e.g., SINCGARS) in support of Marine Corps ground units, tactical aircraft and air control agencies.

(c) Daily changing voice call words/signs should be used when establishing/disestablishing voice communication networks. Although not required after a secure network is established, voice call words/signs provide authentication of authorized users on the network.

<u>1</u>. The use of alphanumeric call words shall be assigned in accordance with the published CEOI/JCEOI.

<u>2</u>. The use of five or 15 letter call signs shall be assigned/coordinated in accordance with reference (x) and the CEOI/JCEOI.

(2) <u>Requests for additions, modifications or deletions to reference (x)</u>

(a) Voice call words/signs are designated for use in establishing and maintaining voice communications. Marine Corps coordination, management and use of daily changing call words/signs are in accordance with reference (x).

(b) The limited number of English words suitable for assignment, which are not obnoxious or ambiguous, has dictated the Joint practice of assigning voice call words/signs at random and without consideration of actual word connotation. Reassignment of voice call words/signs should be necessary only when it is apparent the call word/sign is ambiguous.

(c) Due to the significant scope and difficulty of coordinating call words/signs across Government agencies, DOD and the Military Services, the following submission guidelines are provided:

<u>1</u>. Requests for additions, modifications and deletions to reference (x) shall be forwarded to HQMC C4, via the respective MARFOR, for coordination and deconfliction by the Joint Staff.

<u>2</u>. Requests for additions, modifications or deletions to reference (x) should be submitted in a timely manner. Average required lead-time is 90 to 120 days prior to operational use.

   3. Requests for addition, modification or deletion of call words/signs currently assigned to other Government agencies, DOD or Military Services will not normally be considered.

   4. Requests for addition, modification or deletion of call words/signs currently assigned to Marine Corps organizations is not recommended. However, any such request must include written concurrence and endorsement via the chain-of-command of all affected organizations.

   5. Requesting organizations must provide sufficient justification for the requested addition, modification or deletion.

   6. Requesting organizations must submit the proposed addition or modification within the request.

   7. Proposed call words/signs must be at least five and no more than 15 characters in length to include spaces (Examples: DEVIL, LEATHERNECK or SMEDLEY BUTLER).

   8. Proposed call words/signs must be deconflicted prior to submission and cannot duplicate any call word/sign currently assigned within reference (x).

   9. Requestors are highly encouraged to submit more than one proposal in the event the "first choice" proposal is not available for assignment.

Organization	Abbreviation
Headquarters, US Marine Corps, C4	HQMCC4
US Marine Corps Forces Africa Command	MARFORAF
US Marine Corps Forces Central Command	MARCENT
US Marine Corps Forces Command	MARFORCOM
US Marine Corps Forces European Command	MARFOREUR
US Marine Corps Forces Northern Command	MARFORNORTH
US Marine Corps Forces Pacific Command	MARFORPAC
US Marine Corps Forces Reserve Command	MARFORRES
US Marine Corps Forces Southern Command	MARFORSOUTH
US Marine Corps Forces Special Operations Command	MARSOC
US Marine Corps Forces Strategic Command	MARFORSTRAT
Marine Corps Network Operations and Security Command	MCNOSC
Marine Corps Systems Command	MARCORSYSCOM
Marine Corps Warfighting Lab	MCWL
Training and Education Command	TECOM
Marine Air Ground Task Force Training Command, CA	MAGTFTC
Marine Corps Mountain Warfare Training Center	MCMWTC
Marine Weapons, Training and Tactics Squadron 1	MAWTS1
Marine Corps Communications-Electronics School	MCCES
Marine Corps Installations - East	MCIEAST
Marine Corps Installations - Mid-Pac	MCIMIDPAC
Marine Corps Installations - National Capital Region	MCINCR
Marine Corps Installations - Reserve	MCIRES
Marine Corps Installations - West	MCIWEST
Marine Corps Installations - West-Pac	MCIWESTPAC
Blount Island Command, FL	BLOUNTISCMD
Marine Corps Air Facility Quantico, VA	MCAFQUANTICO
Marine Corps Air Station Beaufort, SC	MCASBEAUFORT
Marine Corps Air Station Cherry Point, NC	MCASCHERRYPT
Marine Corps Air Station Iwakuni, JA	MCASIWAKUNI
Marine Corps Air Station Miramar, CA	MCASMIRAMAR
Marine Corps Air Station New River, NC	MCASNRV
Marine Corps Air Station Yuma, AZ	MCASYUMA
Marine Corps Base Camp Butler, JA	MCBJAPAN
Marine Corps Base Camp Lejeune, NC	MCBCPLEJEUNE
Marine Corps Base Camp Pendleton, CA	MCBCPPENDLETON
Marine Corps Base Hawaii (includes Camp H.M. Smith)	MCBHAWAII
Marine Corps Base Quantico, VA	MCBQUANTICO
Marine Corps Logistics Base Albany, GA	MCLBALBANY
Marine Corps Logistics Base Barstow, CA	MCLBBARSTOW
Marine Corps Recruit Depot Parris Island, SC	MCRDPARRISIS
Marine Corps Recruit Depot San Diego, CA	MCRDSANDIEGO

Figure 3-1. --Marine Corps Standardized
Organizational Abbreviations

Organization	Abbreviation
I Marine Expeditionary Force	IMEF
II Marine Expeditionary Force	IIMEF
III Marine Expeditionary Force	IIIMEF
1st Marine Expeditionary Brigade	1MEB
2nd Marine Expeditionary Brigade	2MEB
3rd Marine Expeditionary Brigade	3MEB
11th Marine Expeditionary Unit	11MEU
13th Marine Expeditionary Unit	13MEU
15th Marine Expeditionary Unit	15MEU
22nd Marine Expeditionary Unit	22MEU
24th Marine Expeditionary Unit	24MEU
26th Marine Expeditionary Unit	26MEU
31st Marine Expeditionary Unit	31MEU
1st Marine Aircraft Wing	1MAW
2nd Marine Aircraft Wing	2MAW
3rd Marine Aircraft Wing	3MAW
4th Marine Aircraft Wing	4MAW
1st Marine Division	1MARDIV
2nd Marine Division	2MARDIV
3rd Marine Division	3MARDIV
4th Marine Division	4MARDIV
1st Marine Logistics Group	1MLG
2nd Marine Logistics Group	2MLG
3rd Marine Logistics Group	3MLG
4th Marine Logistics Group	4MLG
6th Communications Battalion	6COMMBN
7th Communications Battalion	7COMMBN
8th Communications Battalion	8COMMBN
9th Communications Battalion	9COMMBN
1st Marine Special Operations Battalion	1MSOB
2nd Marine Special Operations Battalion	2MSOB
3rd Marine Special Operations Battalion	3MSOB
4th Marine Special Operations Battalion	4MSOB
Marine Special Operations Advisory Group	MSOAG
Marine Special Operations Support Group	MSOSG

Figure 3-1. --Marine Corps Standardized
Organizational Abbreviations (Continued)

Enclosure (1)

Agency   **Data Item 200**

Description   Identifies the agency responsible for managing the
                       frequency assignment.

Input Requirement   Must contain "DON"

Example   200. DON

Unified Command   **Data Item 201**

Description   Identifies the Unified Command or designated
                       representative for the area in which the assignment will be
                       used.

Input Requirement   This item is required for all frequency assignments where
                       either the transmitter or receiver is located outside US&P.
                       Inputs will be determined by the respective regional
                       COCOM policy or guidance.

Unified Command Service   **Data Item 202**

Description   Identifies the service-level organization within the Unified
                       Command area that is responsible for managing the
                       assignment.

Input Requirement   This data item will not normally be used within US&P.
                       However, situations may dictate the use of SFAF data
                       item 202 based on policy or guidance provided by higher
                       headquarters (i. e., USPACOM, USNORTHCOM, etc.).

Example   202. PACOM

Bureau   **Data Item 203**

Description   Required for all Marine Corps frequency assignments
                       worldwide no matter the location.

Input Requirement   Must contain "USMC"

Example   203. USMC

Figure 3-2. --Marine Corps Standardized

SFAF (200 Series) Data Items

Command   **Data Item 204**

Description   Identifies the major command or other applicable
                      organization frequency management level that is
                      subordinate to the responsible Agency identified in SFAF
                      data item 203.

Input Requirement   Authorized entries are "HQMCC4," "MARCORSYSCOM,"
                      "MCNOSC," "MARFORCOM," "MARFORPAC,"
                      "MARSOC," or "MARFORRES" (see Table 3-2).

Example   204. MARFORCOM

Subcommand   **Data Item 205**

Description   Identifies the frequency management level between the
                      command and the installation frequency management
                      office or level that is subordinate to the responsible
                      Agency identified in SFAF data item 204.

Input Requirement   Authorized entries are "IMEF," "IIMEF," "IIIMEF,"
                      "MCINCR," "MCIEAST," "MCIWEST" "MCIRES," or
                      "MCIMIDPAC."

Example   205. IIMEF

Installation Frequency Manager   **Data Item 206**

Description   Identifies the Base, Post, Station or Installation frequency
                      management office responsible for the location of the
                      operating unit.

Input Requirement   Authorized entries are contained in Table 3-2.

Example   206. MCBCPLEJEUNE

Figure 3-2. --Marine Corps Standardized
SFAF (200 Series) Data Items (Continued)

Operating Unit   Data Item 208

Description   Identifies the name or designation of the organization using
                       the frequency assignment.

Input Requirement   Authorized entries are contained in Table 3-2.

Example   207. 2MARDIV

Unit Identification Code   Data Item 208

Description   Identifies the UIC of the operating unit identified in SFAF
                       data item 207.

Input Requirement   Enter the 6-digit UIC starting with the letter designator.

Example   208. M12001

Area AFC/DOD AFC/Other Organizations   Data Item 209

Description   Identifies the service level frequency management office,
                       area AFC, DOD AFC or other organization not provided for
                       in SFAF data items 200-208. Note: SFAF data item 209
                       authorizes up to 10 occurrences.

Input Requirement   First Occurrence – Must contain the respective regional
                       NMCSO. Authorized entries are "NMCSO LANT,"
                       "NMCSO PAC," "NMCSO SOUTHWEST," "NMCSO
                       NORTHWEST," or "NMCSO GUAM."

                       Second Occurrence – Must contain "NMSC"
                       Remaining occurrences will identify and annotate area
                       AFC/DOD AFC or other coordinating organizations in
                       accordance with reference (p).

Example   209. NMCSO LANT
                       209. NMSC
                       209. EAFC

Note: *Some SFAF 200 series data items may require additional data inputs within other
                       data items within the frequency request. Marine Corps OPFOR, installations,
                       organizations and activities shall comply where applicable in accordance with
                       reference (p).*

Figure 3-2. --Marine Corps Standardized
SFAF (200 Series) Data Items (Continued)

FREQUENCY	AUTHORIZED USAGE	STATION CLASS	EMISSION DESIGNATOR	TX POWER	SOURCE
K490	GMDSS/MET AND NAV WARNINGS	MO	1K24F1B	K1	ITU
K500	GMDSS/DISTRESS AND CALLING	MO	20K00A2A	K1	ITU
K518	GMDSS/NAVTEX/MET AND NAV WARNINGS	MO	1K24F1B	K1	ITU
K2174.5	INTL DISTRESS/SAFETY	MO	3K00J3E	K1	ITU
K2182	INTERNATIONAL DISTRESS	MO	6K00A3E	K1	ITU
K2187.5	INTL DISTRESS/SAFETY	MO	3K00J3E	K1	ITU
K3023	INTERNATIONAL SAR	MO	6K00A3E	K1	ITU
K4125	INTERNATIONAL DISTRESS AND SAFETY	MO	6K00A3E	K1	ITU
K4177.5	INTL DISTRESS/SAFETY	MO	3K00J3E	K1	ITU
K4207.5	INTL DISTERSS/SAFETY	MO	3K00J3E	K1	ITU
K4209.5	GMDSS/NAVTEX MET AND NAV WARNINGS	MO	1K24F1B	K1	ITU
K4210	INTL MARITIME NAV SAFETY	MO	6K00A3A	K1	ITU
K5680	INTERNATIONAL SAR	MO	6K00A3E	K1	ITU
K6215	INTERNATIONAL DISTRESS AND SAFETY	MO	6K00A3E	K1	ITU
K6268	INTL DISTRESS/SAFETY	MO	6K00A3E	K1	ITU
K6312	INTL DISTRESS/SAFETY	MO	6K00A3E	K1	ITU
K6314	INTL MARITIME SAFETY/GMDSS	MS	1K24F1B	K1	ITU
K8291	INTL DISTRESS/SAFETY	MO	6K00A3E	K1	ITU
K8364	INTL SAR/SURVIVAL CRAFT	MO	6K00A3E	K1	ITU
K8376.5	INTL DISTRESS/SAFETY	MO	3K00J3E	K1	ITU
K8414.5	INTL DISTRESS/SAFETY	MO	3K00J3E	K1	ITU
K8416.5	GMDSS/INTL MARITIME SAFETY	MS	1K24F1B	K1	ITU
K12290	INTL DISTRESS/SAFETY	MO	6K00A3E	K1	ITU
K12520	INTL DISTRESS/SAFETY	MO	6K00A3E	K1	ITU
K12577	INTL DISTRESS/SAFETY	MO	6K00A3E	K1	ITU
K12579	GMDSS/INTL NAVIGATION SAFETY	MO	1K24F1B	K1	ITU
K16420	INTL DISTRESS/SAFETY	MO	6K00A3E	K1	ITU
K16695	INTL DISTRESS/SAFETY	MO	6K00A3E	K1	ITU
K16804.5	INTL DISTRESS/SAFETY	MO	6K00A3E	K1	ITU
K16806.5	GMDSS/INTL MARITIME SAFETY	MS	1K24F1B	K1	ITU
K19680.5	GMDSS/INTL MARITIME SAFETY	MS	1K24F1B	K1	ITU
K22376	GMDSS/INTL MARITIME SAFETY	MS	1K24F1B	K1	ITU
K26100.5	GMDSS/INTL MARITIME SAFETY	MS	1K24F1B	K1	ITU
M121.5	INTL DISTRESS/AERONAUTICAL EMERGENCY	MO	6K00A3E	W50	ITU
M123.1	INTL EMERGENCY/SAR	MO	6K00A3E	W50	ITU
M156.3	INTL SHIP/AIRCRAFT SAR	MO	25K00G3E	W50	ITU
M156.525	INTL DISTRESS/SAFETY/GMDSS	MO	25K00F3E	W50	ITU
M156.65	INTL SAFETY OF NAVIGATION	MO	25K00F3E	W50	ITU

Figure 3-3. --International Distress and
Emergency Frequencies

Enclosure (1)

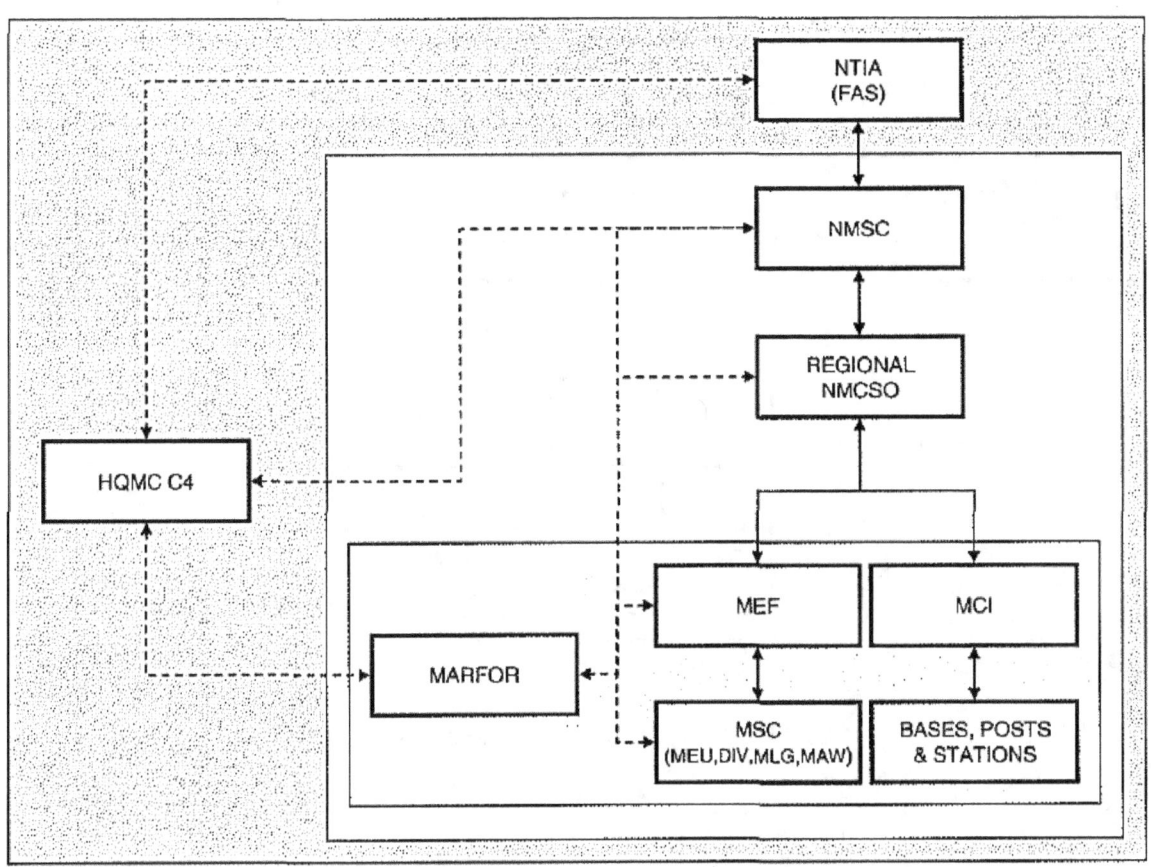

Figure 3-4. --US&P Frequency Request/Assignment Process

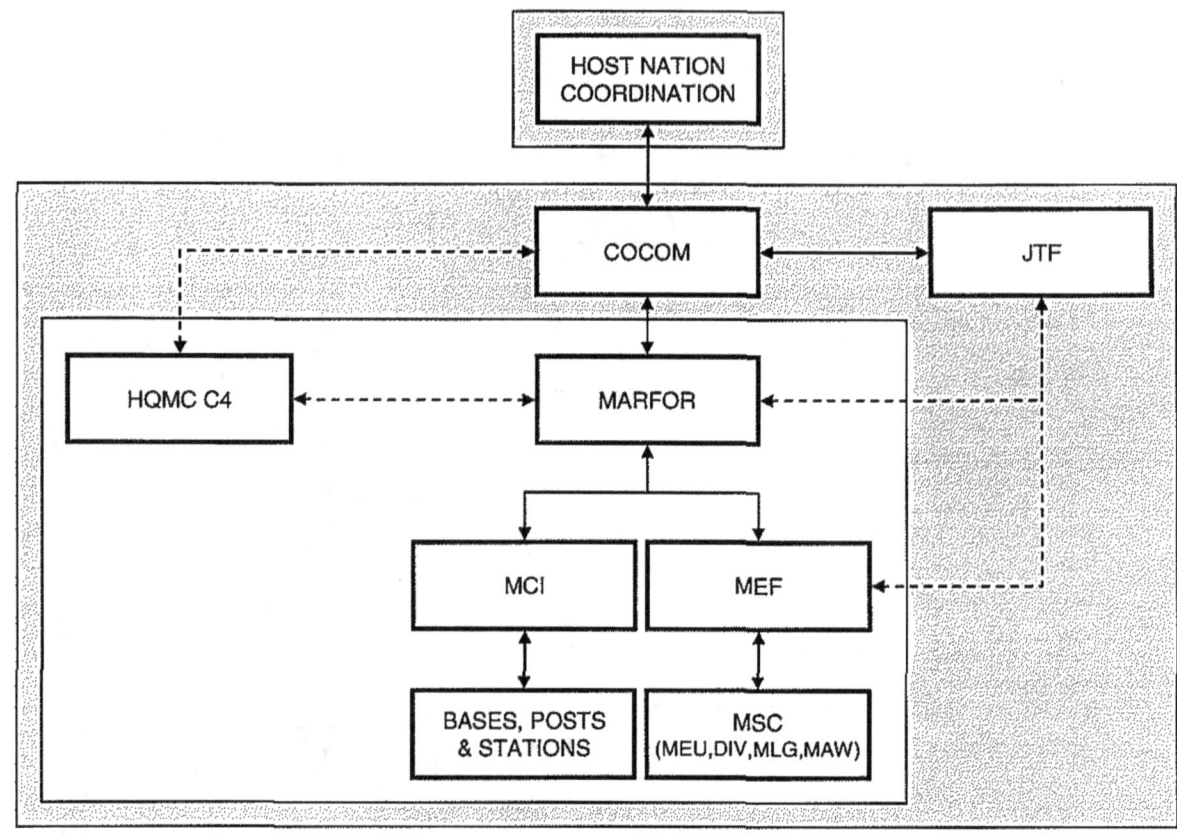

Figure 3-5. --OUS&P Frequency Request/Assignment Process

Chapter 4

Interference Resolution

1. Introduction. The ability to utilize, control and exploit
the electromagnetic spectrum is critical to current and future
Marine Corps operations. Inherent in its control is the timely
and accurate identification, reporting and resolution of
electromagnetic interference (EMI). Interference resolution is
essential to effective command and control (C2) and assured
access to the electromagnetic spectrum by the MAGTF when and
where required. EMI impedes operations and hinders mission
accomplishment by degrading essential equipment and systems that
utilize the electromagnetic spectrum.

    a. EMI is any electromagnetic disturbance that interrupts,
obstructs, degrades or otherwise limits the effective
performance of electronics or electrical equipment to include
S-D equipment and systems.

    b. EMI can be induced intentionally or unintentionally by
numerous friendly, enemy, natural and neutral sources.

2. Joint Spectrum Interference Resolution (JSIR) Program

    a. In accordance with references (u) and (v) the purpose of
the JSIR program is to identify, report and assist in the
resolution of harmful EMI and electronic warfare (EW) to provide
information regarding the reporting and resolution of EMI and
suspected hostile electronic attack (EA) against DOD systems.

        (1) The JSIR program is coordinated and managed by the
Joint Staff, with technical support provided by Joint Spectrum
Center (JSC), designed to be centrally managed with
decentralized execution.

        (2) The JSIR program addresses persistent and recurring
EMI events/incidents during DOD operations; EMI events/incidents
between civil and DOD systems; and EMI involving space systems.

        (3) The JSIR program addresses EMI events/incidents
involving EW/EA affecting DOD S-D equipment and systems.

        (4) Resolution includes, but is not limited to
implementation of EMI corrective actions needed to regain use of
affected spectrum. However, some EMI events/incidents may cease
before corrective action can be taken and in other cases, EMI

corrections may not be feasible, affordable or result in regaining the use of the affected spectrum.

(5) Implementation and costs associated with recommended courses of action (COA) are the responsibility of the affected Service owning/using the S-D equipment or systems.

b. The JSIR process is a three step resolution process for harmful EMI which includes:

(1) Identification, verification, characterization and reporting of EMI events.

(2) Geolocation, analysis, course of action (COA) development and recommendations (corrective action).

(3) Implementation and notification to user(s) and final closure reporting.

c. Marine Corps Operating Forces (OPFOR), installations, organizations and activities will attempt to resolve EMI problems at the lowest possible level in the chain of command. Those incidents that cannot be resolved locally will be referred up the chain of command with resolution attempted at each level.

(1) Detect, report, analyze and attempt to resolve persistent and recurring non-hostile EMI and electronic warfare (EW) incidents affecting DOD systems.

(2) Detect, report, analyze and attempt to resolve suspected hostile electronic attack (EA) against DOD systems (e.g., meaconing, electronic intrusion and jamming).

(a) Meaconing is a form of electromagnetic deception that introduces electromagnetic energy into an enemy's systems that imitates enemy emissions. Meaconing is the intentional transmission of signals designed to deceive users of navigational aids (e.g., tactical air navigation, GPS, non-directional beacons, instrument landing systems, etc.). A more detailed, classified description of meaconing and meaconing effects is located within reference (t).

(b) Electromagnetic intrusion is the intentional insertion of electromagnetic energy into transmission paths in any manner with the objective of deceiving operators or causing confusion. A more detailed, classified description of intrusion and intrusion effects is located within reference (t).

(c) Electromagnetic jamming is the deliberate radiation, re-radiation or reflection of electromagnetic energy for the purpose of preventing or reducing an enemy's effective use of the electromagnetic spectrum with the intent of degrading or neutralizing the enemy's combat capacity. A more detailed, classified description of jamming and jamming effects is located within reference (t).

3. JSIR Reporting Procedures

a. In accordance with references (t), (u) and (v), EMI reporting is mandatory regardless of type, frequency, source or severity.

b. Marine Corps OPFOR, installations, organizations and activities will attempt to resolve EMI at the lowest level in the chain of command using organic and/or other assets available. Those EMI events/incidents that cannot be resolved locally will be referred up the chain of command.

(1) EMI troubleshooting resources for local/operator level EMI resolution are contained in reference (v) and at the JSC JSIR SIPRNET website at https://jdaws.disa.smil.mil.

(2) EMI events/incidents where a source cannot be determined will be forwarded to the Joint Spectrum Center (JSC) operational chain of command for assistance.

(3) Requests for JSC technical support will only be referred via the respective regional COCOM or HQMC C4.

(4) Reporting is mandatory throughout the event/incident and requires submission of the following reports from the onset of and EMI event/incident. The intent of the JSIR process is to pursue EMI through to a successful resolution.

(a) Initial Report

1. The initial report should occur as soon as possible upon suspicion or identification of an EMI event/incident.

2. The initial report should include at least the minimum amount of information that can be determined.

3. The initial report will be in accordance with reference (v).

(b) <u>Supplemental Report</u>

<u>1</u>. Supplemental reports will be submitted as required to provide changes in status, provide additional or essential information, or request for additional resources/ support.

<u>2</u>. Supplemental reports will be in accordance with reference (v).

(c) <u>Final Report</u>. A final, closeout report will be submitted when an EMI event/incident has been resolved, the EMI event/incident has attributed to a hostile emitter or the EMI source cannot be determined.

(5) JSIR reports will be transmitted by official message traffic or e-mail via the SIPRNET no matter the classification.

(6) Classification of EMI reports will be in accordance with the Security Classification Guide and Message Precedence Guidelines contained in reference (v).

(7) JSIR reports shall be maintained in accordance with reference (y) (SSIC 2420.1-4).

Appendix A

Abbreviations and Acronyms

Acronym	Long Title
ADRG	ARC Digitized Raster Graphics
AESOP	Afloat Electromagnetic Spectrum Operations Program
AFC	Area Frequency Coordinator
AOR	Area of Responsibility
APMPWG	Allotment Plan Management Permanent Working Group
APWG	Allied Permanent Working Group
ASD(NII)	Assistant Secretary of Defense for Networks and Information Integration
ASN(RDA)	Assistant Secretary of the Navy (Research, Development and Acquisition)
ATO	Air Tasking Order
C2	Command and Control
CADRG	Compressed ARC Digitized Raster Graphics
CCDR	Combatant Commander
CEOI	Communications-Electronics Operations Instruction
CIB	Controlled Image Base
CIO	Chief Information Officer
CMC	Commandant of the Marine Corps
COA	Courses of Action
COCOM	Combatant Command
COTS	Commercial-off-the-shelf
CREW	Counter RCIED Electronic Warfare (CREW)
DARPA	Defense Advanced Research Projects Agency
DD-1494	Application for Equipment Frequency Allocation
DDA	Designated Disclosure Authority
DIA	Defense Intelligence Agency
DISA	Defense Information Systems Agency
DOC	Department of Commerce
DOD	Department of Defense
DON	Department of the Navy
DSAPWG	Dynamic Spectrum Access Permanent Working Group
DSO	Defense Spectrum Organization
DTED	Digital Terrain Evaluation Data
E3	Electromagnetic Environmental Effects
EA	Executive Agent

EMC	Electromagnetic Compatibility
EME	Electromagnetic Environment
EMI	Electromagnetic Interference
EOB	Electronic Order of Battle
EPS	Emergency Planning Subcommittee
ESG	Expeditionary Strike Group
ESGPWG	Equipment Spectrum Guidance Permanent Working Group
EW/EA	Electronic Warfare/Electronic Attack
FAS	Frequency Assignment Subcommittee
FCC	Federal Communications Commission
FMO	Frequency Management Office
FP	Frequency Panel
FRRS	Frequency Resource Record System
GMF	Government Master File
GOTS	Government-off-the-shelf
GPS	Global Positioning System
HERF	Hazards of Electromagnetic Radiation to Fuel
HERO	Hazards of Electromagnetic Radiation to Ordinance
HERP	Hazards of Electromagnetic Radiation to Personnel
HF	High Frequency
HNA	Host Nation Approval
HNC	Host Nation Coordination
HNSWDO	Host Nation Spectrum World-wide Database Online
HQMC C4	Headquarters, U.S. Marine Corps Command, Control, Communications and Computers
IRAC	Interdepartment Radio Advisory Committee
ISR	Intelligence, Surveillance, and Reconnaissance
IT	Information Technologies
ITU	International Telecommunications Union
ITUPWG	International Telecommunications Union Permanent Working Group
JACS	Joint Automated CEOI System
JCEOI	Joint Communications-Electronics Operating Instruction
JCS	Joint Chiefs of Staff
JDAWS	JSC Database Access Web-server
JETS	Joint Equipment Tactical and Space Database
JFMO	Joint Frequency Management Office
JPO	Joint Program Office
JRFL	Joint Restricted Frequency List
JS	Joint Staff

JSC	Joint Spectrum Center
JSIR	Joint Spectrum Interference Resolution
JSME	Joint Spectrum Management Element
JTF	Joint Task Force
J6	Joint Staff, Director Command, Control, Communications and Computer Systems
MAGTF	Marine Air Ground Task Force
MARCORSYSCOM	Marine Corps Systems Command
MARDIV	Marine Division
MARFOR	U.S. Marine Corps Forces
MARFORCOM	U.S. Marine Corps Forces Command
MARFORPAC	U.S. Marine Corps Forces Pacific
MARFORRES	U.S. Marine Corps Forces Reserve
MARSOC	U.S. Marine Corps Forces Special Operations Command
MAW	Marine Air Wing
MCEB	Military Communications-Electronics Board
MCI	Marine Corps Installations
MCTSSA	Marine Corps Tactical Systems Support Activity
MCWL	Marine Corps Warfighting Lab
MCX	Marine Corps Exchange
MDA	Milestone Decision Authority
MEB	Marine Expeditionary Brigade
MEF	Marine Expeditionary Force
MEU	Marine Expeditionary Unit
MILDEP	Military Department
MLG	Marine Logistics Group
MSC	Major Subordinate Command
NATO	North Atlantic Treaty Organization
NAVAIDS	Navigational Aids
NAVAIR	Naval Air Systems Command
NAVSEA	Naval Sea Systems Command
NERP	NTIA National Emergency Readiness Plan
NETWARCOM	Naval Network Warfare Command
NGIA	National Geospatial Intelligence Agency
NIB	Not-to-Interfere-Basis
NIPRNET	Non-Secure Internet Protocol Router Network
NMCSO	Navy and Marine Corps Spectrum Office
MNL	Master Net List
NMSC	Navy Marine Corps Spectrum Center
NOTAL	Not to, nor required by, all addressees

NTH	Note-to-holder
NTIA	National Telecommunications Information Administration
OMB	Office of Management and Budget
OPFOR	Operating Forces
OPNAVINST	Office of the Chief of Naval Operations Instruction
OPTASKCOM	Operational Tasking Communication Message
OPSEC	Operational Security
OSM	Office of Spectrum Management
O&M	Operations and Maintenance
OUS&P	Outside United States & Possessions
PDA	Principle Designated Disclosure Authority
PM	Program Manager
PO	Program Office
POR	Program of Record
RCA	Radio Communications Assembly
RCIED	Remote Control Improvised Explosive Device
RCS	Radio Conference Subcommittee
RDT&E	Research, Development, Test & Evaluation
RF	Radio Frequency
SATCOM	Satellite Communications
SAR	Satellite Access Request
SCS	Spectrum Certification System
S-D	Spectrum-Dependent
SECDEF	Secretary of Defense
SECNAV	Secretary of the Navy
SECNAVINST	Secretary of the Navy Instruction
SFAF	Standard Frequency Action Format
SINCGARS	Single Channel Ground and Airborne Radio System
SIPRNET	Secure Internet Protocol Router Network
SMAPWG	Spectrum Management Architecture Permanent Working Group
SOPWG	Spectrum Operations Permanent Working Group
SPAWAR	Space & Naval Warfare Systems Command
SPEED	System Planning, Engineering and Evaluation Device
SPO	Strategic Spectrum Office
SPS	Spectrum Planning Subcommittee
SRTM	Shuttle Radar Topography Mission Data
SSPWG	Space Systems Permanent Working Group

SSS	Space Systems Subcommittee
STA	Special Temporary Authorization Assignment
SXXI	Spectrum XXI
TSC	Technical Subcommittee
UAS	Unmanned Aerial System
UN	United Nations
UNS	Universal Needs Statement
USC	United States Code of Federal Regulations
USD(AT&L)	Under Secretary of Defense for Acquisition, Technology and Logistics
USMC	United States Marine Corps
US&P	United States & Possessions
U-UNS	Urgent-Universal Needs Statement
WAN	Wide Area Network
WLAN	Wireless Local Area Network

Appendix B

Glossary of Terms

Electromagnetic Compatibility	The ability of systems, equipment and devices that utilize the electromagnetic spectrum to operate in their intended operational environments without suffering unacceptable degradation or causing unintentional degradation because of electromagnetic radiation or response. It involves the application of sound electromagnetic spectrum management; system, equipment and device design configuration that ensures interference-free operation; and clear concepts and doctrines that maximize operational effectiveness. (JP 1-02)
Electromagnetic Environmental Effects	The impact of the electromagnetic environment upon the operational capability of military forces, equipment, systems and platforms. It encompasses all electromagnetic disciplines, including electromagnetic compatibility and electromagnetic interference; electromagnetic vulnerability; electromagnetic pulse; electronic protection, hazards of electromagnetic radiation to personnel, ordnance, and volatile materials; and natural phenomena effects of lightning and precipitation static. Also called E3. (JP 1-02)

Electromagnetic Environment	The resulting product of the power and time distribution, in various frequency ranges, of the radiated or conducted electromagnetic emission levels that may be encountered by a military force, system or platform when performing its assigned mission in its intended operational environment. It is the sum of electromagnetic interference; electromagnetic pulse; hazards of electromagnetic radiation to personnel, ordnance, and volatile materials; and natural phenomena effects of lightning and precipitation static. Also called EME. (JP 1-02)
Electromagnetic Interference	Any electromagnetic disturbance that interrupts, obstructs or otherwise degrades or limits the effective performance of electronics and electrical equipment. It can be induced intentionally, as in some forms of electronic warfare, or unintentionally, as a result of spurious emissions and responses, intermodulation products, and the like. Also called EMI. (JP 1-02)
Electromagnetic Intrusion	The intentional insertion of electromagnetic energy into transmission paths in any manner with the objective of deceiving operators or causing confusion. (CJCSI 3320.02D)
Electromagnetic Spectrum	The range of frequencies of electromagnetic radiation from zero to infinity. It is divided into 26 alphabetically designed bands. (JP 1-02)

Electronic Attack

That division of electronic warfare involving the use of electromagnetic energy, directed energy, or anti-radiation weapons to attack personnel, facilities or equipment with the intent of degrading, neutralizing or destroying enemy combat capability and is considered a form of fires. Also called EA. EA includes: 1) actions taken to prevent or reduce an enemy's effective use of the electromagnetic spectrum, such as jamming and electromagnetic deception, and 2) employment of weapons that use electromagnetic or directed energy as their primary destructive mechanism (lasers, radio frequency weapons, particle beams). (CJCSM 3212.02B)

Electronic Jamming

The deliberate radiation, re-radiation or reflection of electromagnetic energy for the purpose of preventing or reducing an enemy's effective use of the electromagnetic spectrum and with the intent of degrading or neutralizing the enemy's combat capability. (CJCSI 3320.02D)

Electronic Warfare

Any military action involving the use of electromagnetic and direct energy to control the electromagnetic spectrum or to attack the enemy. Also called EW. The three major subdivisions within electronic warfare are: electronic attack, electronic protection and electronic warfare support. (JP 1-02)

Frequency Assignment

A frequency assignment is an authorization to operate, within prescribed parameters, electronic equipment that emits radio frequency (RF) energy. The authorization contains the assignment's technical parameters and administrative information. (MCEB Pub 7)

Frequency Assignment Record	A frequency assignment record is a grouping of data entries pertaining to an authorized frequency assignment stored within a database. (MCEB Pub 7)
Frequency Deconfliction	A systematic management procedure to coordinate the use of the electromagnetic spectrum for operations, communications and intelligence functions. Frequency deconfliction is one element of electromagnetic spectrum management. (JP 1-02)
Joint Communications-Electronics Operation Instruction	A document that is created to provide the Joint Forces Commander (JFC) the voice and data network architecture to support operations. This document provides the technical characteristics of the net. Also called JCEOI. (CJCSI 3320.03A)
Joint Restricted Frequency List	The JRFL is a time and geographically oriented listing of TABOO, PROTECTED and GUARDED functions, nets, and frequencies. It should be limited to the minimum number of frequencies necessary for friendly forces to accomplish objectives. Also called JRFL. (JP 1-02)
Meaconing	The intentional transmission of signals designed to deceive users of navigational aids, (e.g., tactical air navigation, GPS, non-directional beacons, instrument landing systems, etc.). (CJCSI 3320.02D)
Permanent Assignment	A frequency assignment that is valid for an unspecified period of time (minimum of five years). Also called a "Regular" assignment. (NTIA Manual)

Special Temporary Authorization Assignment	A short-term temporary authorization for Federal users within US&P. STAs are used to support short duration exercises, events or equipment tests and evaluations. (NTIA Manual)
Spectrum Management	Spectrum management consists of planning, coordinating and managing joint use of the electromagnetic spectrum through operational, engineering and administrative procedures. The objective of spectrum management is to enable electronic systems to perform their functions in the intended environment without causing or suffering unacceptable interference. (JP 1-02)
Taboo Frequencies	Any friendly frequency of such importance that it must never be deliberately jammed or interfered with by friendly forces. Normally, these frequencies include international distress, CEASE BUZZER, safety and controller frequencies. These frequencies are generally long standing. However, they may be time-oriented in that, as the combat or exercise situation changes, the restrictions may be removed. (JP 1-02.)
Temporary Assignment	A frequency assignment that is valid for not more than five years and possesses an expiration date. (NTIA Manual)